COMMUNICATING WITH
GRAMMAR
Skills for Life

1

Alice Johnston-Newman

Julita Milewski

OXFORD

UNIVERSITY PRESS

OXFORD
UNIVERSITY PRESS

Oxford University Press is a department of the University of Oxford.
It furthers the University's objective of excellence in research, scholarship,
and education by publishing worldwide. Oxford is a registered trade mark of
Oxford University Press in the UK and in certain other countries.

Published in Canada by
Oxford University Press
8 Sampson Mews, Suite 204,
Don Mills, Ontario M3C 0H5 Canada

www.oupcanada.com

Library and Archives Canada Cataloguing in Publication

Johnston-Newman, Alice, author
Communicating with grammar : skills for life. 1 / Alice
Johnston-Newman & Julita Milewski.

ISBN 978-0-19-900332-7 (pbk.)

1. English language--Grammar.   2. English language--
Textbooks for second language learners.   I. Milewski, Julita,
author   II. Title.

PE1112.J64 2014   428.2'4   C2012-905795-9

Cover image: Barrett & MacKay/ALL CANADA PHOTOS INC.

Oxford University Press is committed to our environment.
Wherever possible, our books are printed on paper
which comes from responsible sources.

Printed and bound in Canada

1 2 3 4 — 17 16 15 14

AUTHORS

Authors

Alice Johnston-Newman, BA, MA, CTESL, is a language teacher, writer, and translator with close to 30 years' experience teaching English as a first and second language to Canadians, new Canadians, and international students. She is currently a professor at La Cité collégiale in Ottawa and has taught at Algonquin College, Carleton University, and abroad. During her professional career, she has created and adapted teaching material and student workbooks for ESL, enriched level, as well as specialized, career-oriented English courses. She also collaborated with two of the other *Communicating with Grammar* authors in the publication of *Famous Canadian Authors Developing English Skills* (Pearson, 2007), a reading and vocabulary building text for intermediate and advanced ESL learners.

Julita Milewski, BA, M.Ed, has been an ESL teacher for the last 13 years. Her desire to teach ESL started as she herself was learning English as a second language when she first immigrated to Canada as a teenager. Her teaching experience includes working with adolescent and adult learners, international students, and immigrants. She has taught at the University of Ottawa, Carleton University, and various private language schools. She is currently an ESL professor at La Cité collégiale in Ottawa.

Series Team

The whole author team created the approach, the topics covered, and the chapter structure for the three-level series *Communicating with Grammar: Skills for Life*. Though each level has its specific lead author or authors, the team worked collaboratively in the development of these publications.

Mohammad Hashemi, BA, MA, is a teacher, editor, translator, and author. He has been coordinating and teaching English for more than 20 years, formerly at Carleton University and Algonquin College. He currently teaches at La Cité collégiale in Ottawa, Ontario. For more information about Mohammad visit his website at www.mohammadhashemi.com.

Silvija Kalnins, BA, CTESL, has been teaching and coordinating English for the past 10 years at La Cité collégiale. This is her third career. As the eldest daughter of Latvian immigrants, she has experienced first-hand the difficulties of English language acquisition, which has sensitized her to the needs and challenges that her students face.

Jaklin Zayat, BA (Modern Languages), M.Ed, has been teaching ESL and academic writing for over 20 years. She speaks five languages and is recognized for her knowledge of the construction of many other languages. She currently teaches at La Cité Collégiale and the University of Ottawa. A co-author of *Famous Canadian Authors*, she also enjoys writing stories for future publications.

Acknowledgements

From the Authors

We would like to thank our colleagues for their help and feedback during this project. We especially want to thank our families and friends for their enormous support, understanding, and encouragement from the project's start to its very completion. Special thanks also go to the excellent editorial and publishing team at OUP Canada for their professional advice and greatly appreciated assistance during the writing of this book. Finally, we want to acknowledge each other—we have enjoyed a very mutually supportive, creative experience as a team.

Reviewers

Oxford University Press Canada would like to express appreciation to the instructors and coordinators who graciously offered feedback on *Communicating with Grammar* at various stages of the developmental process. Their feedback was instrumental in helping to shape and refine the series.

Gill Atkinson	Camosun College
Roisin Dewart	Université du Québec à Montréal
Susan Drolet	Cégep Garneau
Barbara Fraser	Collège Ahuntsic
Daniela Geremia	
Brandie Glasgow-Spanos	Niagara Catholic District School Board: St. Ann Adult Learning Centre
Emrah Görgülü	Simon Fraser University
Therese Gormley Hirmer	Humber College Institute of Technology & Advanced Learning
Kristina Gryz	Red River College
Corinne Hamel-Taylor	S.U.C.C.E.S.S.
Eva Ing	George Brown College
Rob Inouye	Simon Fraser University
Maureen Kelbert	Vancouver Community College
Kristibeth Kelly	Fanshawe College
Kara King-Barratt	Catholic Crosscultural Services
Izabella Kojic-Sabo	University of Windsor
Claire La Fleur	The Centre for Skills Development and Training
Anita Lemonis	Vancouver Community College
Sandra Madigan	Southeast Regional College
Corinne Marshall	Fanshawe College
Lara McInnis	Humber College
Jennifer Peachey	VanWest College
Mark Rankin	
Brett Reynolds	Humber College
Cheri Rohloff	The University of Winnipeg
Wilfried Schuster	Toronto District School Board: Adult Ed
Adrianna Semerjian	City Adult Learning Centre
Marti Sevier	Simon Fraser University

CONTENTS

Chapter 8
Word Choice, Word Pairs   125

Part 2 Review   141

PART 3

Chapter 9
Simple Future—*Will* and *Be Going To*   147

Chapter 10
Modals   163

INTRODUCTION

Welcome to Communicating with Grammar!

Communicating with Grammar: Skills for Life is a Canadian series for ESL and EFL students looking to improve their understanding of English grammar. Offering grammar instruction through the use of the four skills—reading, writing, listening, and speaking—the series helps students internalize concepts for better use in all their communication. Students improve their command of English grammar through a broad spectrum of activities that set them up for further study or work in an English-speaking environment.

The ***Communicating with Grammar*** series employs a task-based and communicative methodology. Using a "learn–practise–use in context" approach, the books deliver the essential grammar concepts via practical exercises and activities, helping learners become functional in English as quickly and efficiently as possible. The communicative activities then help students internalize the grammar in context.

Series Features

This Canadian series guides student learning by combining a communicative task-based approach with discrete grammar instruction using traditional exercises. It provides warm-up activities, explicit grammar teaching, considerable use of practical example sentences, and a combination of mechanical and interactive exercises. The more traditional exercises allow students to practise each concept, while engaging communicative activities further reinforce the grammar being studied. Moreover, the target grammar is embedded in the reading, listening, and writing sections that follow, facilitating further grammar use in context. Additionally, review units provide, at regular intervals, an opportunity for students to practise the material and solidify the key aspects of their learning. The books have the additional advantage of providing flexibility for those learners who thrive on extra challenge while maintaining the intended level of the target material.

Chapter Structure

Chapters are logically organized into an overview, a series of grammar topics with practice, a cumulative section incorporating all four skill areas, and a summary. Grammar is treated as a necessary component of all four skill areas, and students are encouraged to use the focal grammar topic with each of these skills in every chapter.

Overview

Each chapter opens with a very brief explanation of the chapter's grammar topic, followed by a **Warm-up** activity that engages students and provides an opportunity to start thinking about and using the target grammar in context. Given a real-life task, students are encouraged to use the new grammar concept to communicate with their classmates.

Grammar

The chapter's target grammar is divided into logical and manageable parts, each of which uses a learn–practice–use in context approach.

The grammar instruction starts with a **Formation** (learn) section that offers a clear explanation of the grammar topic, often by using tables and charts, and illustrates the mechanics in context.

Exercises (practice) follow the grammar explanation. A series of traditional drills gives students controlled exposure to the language structures and deals with common difficulties faced by most learners. The exercises are varied and include sentence completion, sentence construction, matching, ordering, error correction, transformation, multiple choice, fill in the blanks, and more.

Further practice through interactive **Communicative Activities** (use in context) allows students to apply the new grammar topic in a practical manner. These engaging tasks, which include class, pair, and group activities, enable learners to communicate in an authentic way by using the grammar they have learned.

Bringing It All Together

This key section at the heart of the chapter provides an opportunity for students to bring together all the chapter's grammar parts and apply them in a more authentic context. It includes a number of additional **Communicative Activities** that challenge students to incorporate all aspects of the chapter's grammar. The **Reading** section contains both a reading passage and comprehension questions, requiring students to apply the chapter's grammar points. The audio clips and comprehension questions in the **Listening** section again facilitate input and output of the target grammatical structures. In the **Writing** section, students are provided with another productive opportunity to apply the grammar, this time in a longer piece of writing.

Chapter Review

Each chapter's review section opens with a helpful **Summary** of all aspects of the grammar taught in the chapter; students can check their learning through a complete and convenient chapter grammar reference. The traditional **Exercises** that follow are designed to give additional straightforward practice for students to work on independently in class or for homework.

Appendices and Glossary

To supplement and support the learning, each book ends with quick-reference appendices, with additional information on grammar points or usage, and a glossary of all key vocabulary from the chapters' Readings.

Three Levels

Level 1 is designed for students with basic English who still need to build a solid foundation of the major verb tenses and sentence structure. Students learn to formulate more accurate sentences and questions through the grammar lessons and exercises. They expand their English vocabulary through the Reading and Listening components. This level also focuses on targeting the common basic grammatical errors students may still need to learn how to correct.

Level 2 is designed for students who have completed Level 1 or who have enough grammar and a basic understanding of the four skills to formulate questions in English and construct more-complex sentences. At the entry into this level, students can usually clearly communicate their intentions to others but still make frequent errors in structure, tense, and usage that may slow comprehension. Level 2 focuses on improving grammar in the four skills areas to an exit level at which students will have more fluency, a larger vocabulary, and the ability to express themselves by using more complicated sentence structures.

Level 3 is the bridging level to fluency in English usage. This level completes all the perfect verb tenses and has chapters on the active and passive voice and reported speech. It further develops students' ability to construct more-complex sentences with the study of clauses. Reading and Listening components are from authentic sources, preparing students for real-world communication. At the completion of this level, students will have the confidence to communicate with native speakers academically or professionally.

Additional Series Components

- **Audio CDs** are available for each level in the series. They contain either authentic or constructed listening clips, depending on the level and grammar topic.
- The **online Teacher Resource** contains teaching notes and aids, additional communicative activities and exercises to be used as practice or in a test setting, audio transcripts, and an answer key for the exercises and the reading and listening comprehension questions.

Parts of Speech, Numbers, Nouns, and Pronouns

OVERVIEW

- There are some basic things to know about a language in order to learn it more easily.
- Understanding the parts of speech, numbers, nouns, articles, and *there is / there are* helps you start using the English language more quickly and easily.

PARTS OF SPEECH

Learning the parts of speech helps you understand and use the parts of a sentence correctly.

Warm-up

Work in pairs. Read the sentences below. Pay special attention to the underlined word in each sentence. Does the word present

- an action?
- a person or a thing?
- more information about another word?
- a location?
- a link between two ideas in the sentence?

Frank <u>drives</u> a bus.   *drives* = action

1. They sing in a <u>choir</u>.

2. The man is <u>in</u> the car.

3. Mary <u>plays</u> the guitar.

4. I have a brother <u>and</u> a sister.

5. The sun is very <u>warm</u> today.

Formation

Part of Speech	Use	Examples
verb (v.)	expresses an action or a state	John **walks** to school. John **is** tall.
noun (n.)	names a person, place, or thing	**John** walks to **school**.
article (art.)	limits a noun *A* and *an* are singular and not specific. Use *a* before consonant sounds and *an* before vowel sounds. *The* is specific and can be singular or plural.	**a** book **an** apple **the** book**s** on **the** table
adjective (adj.)	modifies or qualifies a noun or pronoun	the **black** cat John is **tall**. **This** book is **new**.
adverb (adv.)	modifies or qualifies a verb, an adjective, or an adverb	John walks **quickly**. John is **really** tall. John walks **very quickly**.

pronoun (pron.)	replaces a noun	I, you, he, she, it, we, they: **I** see a book. me, you, him, her, it, us, them: She knows **them**.
preposition (prep.)	shows a link between words for place, time, direction, origin, etc.	at, on, in, to, from, for, above: The book is **on** the table.
conjunction (conj.)	creates a link between parts of a sentence There are coordinating conjunctions and subordinating conjunctions.	coordinating conjunctions: and, but, so, or: The students **and** the teacher are in the room. subordinating conjunctions: before, after, when, because: She takes the bus **when** it is cold.

 # COMMUNICATIVE ACTIVITY 1

Let's Identify

Work in pairs. Identify the part of speech of each word in the following sentences.

    noun   art.   prep.
Maya rides a bike to school.
         verb   noun   noun

1. The students study in the library after class.

   the   _____article_____

   students _____

   study   _____

   in   _____

   the   _____

   library   _____

   after   _____

   class   _____

2. Frank and I are best friends.

   Frank   _____

   and   _____

   I   _____

   are   _____

   best   _____

   friends   _____

3. He lives in a very small apartment.

   He   _____

   lives   _____

   in   _____

   a   _____

   very   _____

   small   _____

   apartment _____

4. That teacher reads slowly and clearly.

   that   _____

   teacher   _____

   reads   _____

   slowly   _____

   and   _____

   clearly   _____

NUMBERS

Numbers help us get and give necessary information about ourselves and our lives. We use them to give personal information, to tell the time, to find out the cost of something, and so on.

Warm-up

In the following word search puzzle, find and (circle) the numbers in the list below. The words only go left to right → and top to bottom ↓. The number "one" is already circled for you.

T	T	T	H	R	E	E	I	G	H	T	W	O	E
E	S	I	X	E	F	O	R	T	Y	-	S	I	X
L	N	E	T	S	I	X	T	Y	-	T	W	O	E
E	I	I	E	I	F	E	H	I	N	H	F	V	T
V	N	G	N	X	T	I	I	E	Y	I	O	N	F
E	E	H	S	T	Y	G	R	T	F	R	U	I	I
N	T	T	E	E	-	H	T	W	O	T	R	N	F
S	Y	Y	V	E	F	T	E	E	R	Y	T	E	T
E	-	T	E	N	I	E	E	N	T	-	E	T	E
V	N	W	N	S	V	E	N	T	Y	F	E	E	E
E	I	E	T	W	E	N	T	Y	-	O	N	E	N
N	N	L	E	T	H	I	R	T	Y	U	T	N	I
S	E	V	E	N	T	Y	-	T	H	R	E	E	N
(O	N	E)	N	F	I	V	E	F	O	U	R	I	E

~~one~~	eleven	twenty-one
two	twelve	thirty
three	thirteen	thirty-four
four	fourteen	forty
five	fifteen	forty-six
six	sixteen	fifty-five
seven	seventeen	sixty-two
eight	eighteen	seventy-three
nine	nineteen	eighty
ten	twenty	ninety-nine

Formation

Cardinal numbers show quantity; we count with them. Ordinal numbers show the order of things, not the quantity.

Cardinal Numbers		Ordinal Numbers	
1	one	1st	first
2	two	2nd	second
3	three	3rd	third
4	four	4th	fourth
5	five	5th	fifth
6	six	6th	sixth
7	seven	7th	seventh

Cardinal Numbers		Ordinal Numbers	
8	eight	8th	eighth
9	nine	9th	ninth
10	ten	10th	tenth
11	eleven	11th	eleventh
12	twelve	12th	twelfth
13	thirteen	13th	thirteenth
14	fourteen	14th	fourteenth
15	fifteen	15th	fifteenth
16	sixteen	16th	sixteenth
17	seventeen	17th	seventeenth
18	eighteen	18th	eighteenth
19	nineteen	19th	nineteenth
20	twenty	20th	twentieth
21	twenty-one	21st	twenty-first
22	twenty-two	22nd	twenty-second
30	thirty	30th	thirtieth
40	forty	40th	fortieth
50	fifty	50th	fiftieth
60	sixty	60th	sixtieth
70	seventy	70th	seventieth
80	eighty	80th	eightieth
90	ninety	90th	ninetieth
100	one hundred	100th	one hundredth
101	one hundred and one	101st	one hundred and first
110	one hundred and ten	110th	one hundred and tenth
200	two hundred	200th	two hundredth
300	three hundred	300th	three hundredth
1000	one thousand	1000th	one thousandth
1500	one thousand five hundred or fifteen hundred	1500th	one thousand five hundredth or fifteen hundredth
3300	three thousand three hundred or thirty-three hundred	3300th	three thousand three hundredth or thirty-three hundredth
10,000	ten thousand	10,000th	ten thousandth
1,000,000	one million	1,000,000th	one millionth

All languages have patterns. Learn the patterns, and the language becomes easier to learn and use.

- *One*, *two*, and *three* and their combinations have their own patterns for the ordinal numbers; all the other numbers just add -th.
- Spelling: When the number ends in a consonant and *y*, change the *y* to *i* before adding the ending -*eth*. We add the *e* to make the ending easier to pronounce.
- We commonly group numbers in pairs when we say them for money, years, and telephone numbers.
  - We usually say *1983* as "nineteen eighty-three."
  - We can say *742-2690* as the individual numbers, but we often group the last four numbers in pairs: "seven four two, twenty-six ninety."

MONTHS OF THE YEAR

January	May	September
February	June	October
March	July	November
April	August	December

Numbers are also part of the formation of dates. There are a few ways to express dates. How we say them and write them differ also.

Written Dates	Spoken Dates
February 10, 2014	February the tenth, 2014
the 10th of February, 2014	the tenth of February, 2014
02/10/14, (02-10-14)	the tenth of February, 2014 the tenth of the second month of 2014
14/02/10, 2014/02/10, (14-02-10, 2014-02-10)	February the tenth, 2014

The first two written dates are more formal, and we use them in correspondence. We use the numerical versions on application forms, for example.

EXERCISE 1

🔊 Track 01

Listen to the audio. Answer the questions.

Conversation 1

1. What is Ms. London's phone number?
   a) 545-6215
   b) 545-6250
   c) 445-6250

2. What is the work order number?
   a) B1423S19
   b) B4023S19
   c) B1423S90

3. How much is the repair bill?
   a) $70.87
   b) $77.87
   c) $72.87

Conversation 2

1. How much cash do the speakers have? _____

2. What is the phone number of the pizza place? _____

3. What is the total cost of the pizza? _____

4. What is the street number of their address? _____

5. What is their phone number? _____

Conversation 3

1. What is Mr. Powers's bank card number? _____

2. Write his date of birth. _____

3. What is the date of his anniversary? _____

TELLING TIME

We also use numbers for telling the time. There are two ways to say the time: traditional and digital.

It is three o'clock.
3:00: It is three.

It is ten past seven.
7:10: It is seven ten.

It is a quarter after ten.
10:15: It is ten fifteen.

For the first 30 minutes of the hour, we say "past" or "after" the hour. For the second 30 minutes or half hour, we say "to" the next hour.

It is half past twelve.
12:30: It is twelve thirty.

It is twenty-five to nine.
8:35: It is eight thirty-five.

It is a quarter to four.
3:45: It is three forty-five.

It is midnight.
12:00 a.m.
It is twelve at night.

It is noon.
12:00 p.m.
It is twelve in the afternoon.

For specific times, use *at*. For periods of time, use *in*, except with *night*.

I go to work **at** 9:00 (at nine o'clock) **in** the morning.

We visit friends **in** the evening.

John works **at** night.

EXERCISE 2

Write the following times in both forms.

11:24   **It is twenty-four past eleven.**

               It is eleven twenty-four.

1. 6:30 _____

_____

2. 1:40 _____

_____

3. 8:15 _____

_____

4. 2:45 _____

_____

5. 12:50 _____

_____

COMMUNICATIVE ACTIVITY 2

What Time Is It?

Work in teams. Your teacher will show you a card with a time in number form on it. The first player of Team A says the time out loud. The second player writes it in word form on the board. If they are both right, their team gets two points. If they are wrong, Team B has the chance to earn the missed points.

NOUNS: COUNTABLE AND NON-COUNTABLE NOUNS AND PLURALS

English has two main kinds of nouns in English: countable and non-countable. Countable nouns have plural forms; non-countable nouns have no plural forms.

Warm-up

Work in pairs. Read the following passage and <u>underline</u> all the nouns. Are the nouns in the passage things or items that you can count? Are they ideas or categories of things? Write them in the correct columns below.

> The students in this class enjoy playing games. The teacher thinks these activities help the students learn English more quickly. Every day, they spend some time doing activities that use the language. They have fun. They also practise the lessons and gain confidence.

Things or People You Can Count		Abstract Ideas or Categories
1.	6.	1.
2.	7.	2.
3.	8.	3.
4.	9.	4.
5.	10.	

Formation

Countable nouns have plural forms; we can count them.

one boy → two boys   one book → two books   one table → two tables

Non-countable nouns have no plural forms; we cannot count them. We can divide them into the kinds shown in the charts below.

Categories of Items		Abstract Ideas and Mass Nouns	
clothing	mail	advice	knowledge
equipment	money	beauty	love
furniture	music	soil	luck
homework	news	evidence	research
jewellery	software	experience	sand
luggage or baggage	tourism	fun	time
machinery	work	health	violence
		information	weather

Certain Food and Drink Categories		Names of Languages and Proper Names	Academic Subjects
bread	pasta	Chinese	biology
butter	poultry	English	history
cheese	sugar	French	mathematics
coffee	tea	Spanish	physics
meat	water	Mary	politics
milk	wine	Frank	science

A few non-countable nouns can also be countable nouns, but their meanings usually change.

I have a lot of **work** to do. The museum has many beautiful **works** of art.

- Abstract nouns are concepts, feelings, or things we can't touch.
- Mass nouns are substances, such as sand, smoke, or butter. We can touch them, but we cannot count them.
- Proper nouns are the specific names or titles of people and things. Proper nouns always have a capital letter. For example,

  Lake Ontario is a very large lake.

  Lake Ontario is a proper noun because it is the name of a specific lake. The second lake in the sentence is a common noun because it means a body of water in general.

- Non-countable nouns are always singular even if they end in an s: for example, news, politics.

  The news is good.

  The news is on TV at 6:00 p.m.

  Physics is my favourite science subject.

NOUNS—PLURAL FORMS

Nouns Ending in	Plural Spelling	Examples
most consonants and silent *e*	+ *s*	bands, cats, dogs, books, computers houses, suitcases, blouses
a consonant + *y*	change *y* to *i* + *es*	city: cities; baby: babies
a vowel + *y*	+ *s*	boys, plays, bays
a consonant + *o*	+ *es*	hero: heroes, echo: echoes (except musical terms and shortened words + *s*: pianos, photos)

other vowels (not *o*)	+ *s*	bananas, skis
two vowels	+ *s*	radios, videos
s, x, z, ch, sh	+ *es*	buses, boxes, buzzes, watches, bushes (to make them easier to pronounce)
f or *fe*	+ *s* change *f* to *v* + *es*	chefs, chiefs wife: wives; life: lives, leaf: leaves (There is no regular pattern.)

Irregular Plurals

Some plural forms remain from Old English and do not follow the rules in the previous chart.

Singular	child	foot	goose	man	mouse	person	tooth	woman
Plural	children	feet	geese	men	mice	people	teeth	women

Some other nouns don't change but are still countable nouns. The most common are certain species: sheep, fish, deer, salmon, moose, trout.

He has 100 sheep. I saw a sheep in the garden.

EXERCISE 3

Write four plural countable nouns for each non-countable noun category.

mail: letters, parcels, bills, flyers

1. food _____

2. equipment _____

3. furniture _____

4. jewellery _____

5. money _____

EXERCISE 4

Write the plural forms of the nouns. If the noun does not have a plural form, put X in the blank.

1.	horse	_____	11. information	_____
2.	tomato	_____	12. truck	_____
3.	woman	_____	13. life	_____
4.	money	_____	14. radio	_____
5.	city	_____	15. bicycle	_____
6.	child	_____	16. toy	_____
7.	homework	_____	17. deer	_____
8.	piano	_____	18. foot	_____
9.	house	_____	19. mouse	_____
10.	fax	_____	20. ash	_____

Pronunciation of the -s Ending

To make pronunciation easier, there are three ways to pronounce the *-s* ending of plural nouns. Whether we say the /s/, the /z/, or the /iz/ sound depends on the final sound of the singular noun. Remember it is the **sound** that matters, not the written letter.

Use the Sound	When the Final Sound of the Singular Noun Is	Examples
/s/	one of these voiceless consonant sounds: f, k, p, t, th (as in *with*)	chef: chefs (chef/s/) book: books (book/s/) mop: mops (mop/s/) cat: cats (cat/s/) bath: baths (bath/s/)
/z/	a **vowel sound** or one of these voiced consonant sounds: b, d, g, j, l, m, n, ng, r, v, th (as in *then*)	tomato: tomatoes (tomato/z/) banana: bananas (banana/z/) cab: cabs (cab/z/) dog: dogs (dog/z/) doll: dolls (doll/z/) ring: rings (ring/z/)
/iz/	one of these consonant sounds: s, x, ch, sh, z, zh	bus: buses (bus/iz/) box: boxes (box/iz/) watch: watches (watch/iz/) bush: bushes (bush/iz/) buzz: buzzes (buzz/iz/) edge: edges (edge/iz/)

EXERCISE 5

 Track 02

Listen to the audio. Write each plural noun you hear in the correct column, based on the pronunciation of the -s ending.

/s/	/z/	/iz/

COMMUNICATIVE ACTIVITY 3

Countable or Non-countable?

Work in teams. Your teacher will provide a worksheet with 20 nouns. Write the nouns in the correct column: countable or non-countable. If the noun is countable, write the plural form as well. The team that finishes first with the correct answers wins.

ARTICLES AND DETERMINERS

Articles and other determiners introduce nouns and tell us if they are singular or plural; indefinite, definite (or specific), or general; and countable or non-countable.

Warm-up

Work in pairs. Read the following passage. Underline all the nouns. What do you notice about the words that come immediately before the nouns?

Francisco is a student. He studies English at the college. There are many students in the class. Some students want to take courses at the college when they finish the English course. Francisco wants to go to a university to study medicine. He wants to become a doctor. That takes much time and effort.

The indefinite articles *a* and *an* introduce a singular, countable noun that we don't know anything about yet. The definite article *the* introduces a specific noun, something that is known.

> There is **a** dog in the yard. (There is no specific information about the dog.)

> **The** dog is looking for its ball. (The dog is now a specific dog.)

The first time something is mentioned, use *a* or *an*; the second time, use *the*.

Formation

Article or Determiner	Definite / Indefinite	Singular / Plural	Countable / Non-countable	Examples
a (before a consonant sound)	indefinite	singular	countable nouns	a cat
an (before a vowel sound)	indefinite	singular	countable nouns	an umbrella
the	definite (specific)	singular or plural	countable and non-countable nouns	the cat the cats the furniture
some	indefinite	plural	countable and non-countable nouns	I have some books. I have some money.
Ø (no article)	general	plural	countable and non-countable nouns	Cats are smart. Knowledge is power.

Do not use articles with

- languages: He speaks Russian.
- sports: I like hockey.
- names of countries, provinces or territories, or states that are singular: We live in Canada.

Exception: Use *the* with plural or qualified names of countries, provinces or territories, or states: the United States, the Philippines, the Republic of China, the Northwest Territories.

Other Determiners

Determiner	Used with Countable Nouns	Used with Non-countable Nouns	Example Sentences
much		✓	I don't have much time.
many	✓		It takes many years to become a doctor.
a little		✓	I have a little money.
a few	✓		I have a few dollars.
a lot of	✓	✓	I don't have a lot of time. It takes a lot of years to become a doctor.

EXERCISE 6

Fill in the blanks with *a*, *an*, *the*, *some*, or Ø (nothing).

1. Two of _____ students in my class come from _____

   France.

2. John is _____ good hockey player. He plays _____

   hockey for _____ college team.

3. It is nice to have _____ break between _____ classes.

   We have _____ hour to relax.

4. I need to buy _____ furniture for my new apartment. I need

   _____ desk, _____ table, and _____

   chairs. I also need _____ alarm clock.

5. Amanda is really interested in _____ politics. She watches

   _____ news every day.

EXERCISE 7

Circle the letter of the correct word or phrase to complete the sentences.

1. How _____ homework do you have tonight?
   a) a little
   b) many
   c) much

2. Susan has _____ photos of her family.
   a) a few of
   b) a lot of
   c) much

3. The museum has _____ interesting exhibits.
   a) much
   b) many
   c) a little

4. How _____ does this shirt cost?
   a) much
   b) many
   c) a little

5. I have _____ exercises to finish for homework.
   a) a little
   b) a few
   c) much

THERE IS, THERE ARE

The structure *there + be* introduces information. *There is* introduces singular and non-countable nouns. *There are* introduces plural nouns.

Use	Form	Keywords	Example Sentences
to introduce singular or non-countable nouns	There is	a, an, the, some, much, a little, one	There is a book on the table. There is some money in my wallet. There is a little time before class.
to introduce plural nouns	There are	the, some, many, few, two, three, etc.	There are some books on the table. There are many students in the class.

Warm-up

Look around the classroom. On a separate sheet of paper, make a chart like the one below. List the things and people you see. Use the correct column. Compare your list with your classmates' lists.

There is . . .	There are . . .
a teacher	12 students

Formation

Positive	Negative	Question
There + is / are + noun / noun phrase	*There + is / are* + not + noun / noun phrase	*Is / Are + there* + noun / noun phrase
There is a book on the table.	There isn't a book on the table.	Is there a book on the table?
There is **some** money in my wallet.	There isn't **any** money in my wallet.	Is there **any** money in my wallet?
There are **some** books on the table.	There aren't **any** books on the table.	Are there **any** books on the table?
There are many students in the class.	There aren't many students in the class.	Are there many students in the class?

Look at the noun that follows the structure *there is / are*. If it is plural, use *are*.

The indefinite article *some* usually changes to *any* in negative and question formations.

EXERCISE 8

Fill in the blanks with *is* or *are*.

1. There _____ many people in the restaurant.

2. _____ there some information about the art exhibit online?

3. There _____ a birthday party tonight for Mariko.

4. There _____ a lot of good movies playing this week.

5. _____ there an assignment to do for English class for tomorrow?

COMMUNICATIVE ACTIVITY 4

Editing

Work in pairs. There are five errors with the structure *there is / there are* in the following passage. Find and correct them. (Hint: Sometimes it helps to read aloud when looking for errors.)

Hi, Paul

How's college? I'm really enjoying my school. There are lots of social activities so you can get to know other students. There are many clubs and sports teams too. Is there many things to do at your school? How are your courses? Are you enjoying them?

I really like mine, but I am so busy and stressed. There are eight courses to take each semester. Most of them are okay, but there is a couple of courses that are really heavy. For example, there is a lot of homework to do for the communications course. There is at least five projects to do before the end of the semester. There are so much to do. I don't know if there are enough time to do all that work and the work in my other courses.

I hope your courses are going well. Talk to you soon.

Jan

BRINGING IT ALL TOGETHER

COMMUNICATIVE ACTIVITY 5

Role-Play

Work in pairs. Take turns role-playing the different situations. Then perform them in front of the class.

Situation A: Telephone the dentist's office to make an appointment because you have a toothache.

Situation B: Ask the clerk in a store for the price of printer ink. Tell the clerk the make of the printer or the number of the ink cartridge.

Situation C: You want to arrange to meet your friend for a coffee. Leave a message. Mention the time, the place, and your phone number.

Situation D: You want to get more information about a used car (or something else) that's for sale. Call the number and ask questions.

COMMUNICATIVE ACTIVITY 6

Spelling Bee

Work in teams. Your teacher will read a noun. A member of Team A writes the plural form on the board. If the spelling is correct, that team scores a point. If not, Team B gets a chance to spell it correctly and steal a point. Your teacher will then read another noun for Team B. The team with the most points wins.

Reading

Read the email and answer the questions that follow.

STARTING COLLEGE

Hi, Sam

I just want to let you know that I'm beginning to get used to college. It's sure a bit crazy at first. It is definitely a lot different from high school.

When you first start your studies at college, there is a lot of information to take

in. They give you so much <u>stuff</u> to read. Before you start your classes, there is so much to do and so many <u>lineups</u> to wait in. First, you need to <u>register</u> and pay your <u>tuition fees</u>. Each program has specific courses you need to take. Then you get to choose your optional courses. The next step is to print out your class schedule. It's a good idea to <u>become familiar with</u> the <u>campus</u>. It's important to know where the classrooms are before your classes start. I try not to get lost, but it's <u>confusing</u> sometimes.

I start my classes tomorrow morning at 8:00 and I don't finish until 7:00 in the evening. Plus, I need to buy my textbooks tomorrow. I'm really busy, kind of nervous, but really excited all at the same time.

Talk to you later.
Joe

COMPREHENSION

1. Does Joe think college is the same as high school?

   _____

2. Where does Joe say you need to wait?

   _____

3. What does Joe say you need to do first, second, and third?

   _____

4. Why is it important to become familiar with the college campus?

   _____

5. What words or phrases does Joe use to describe how he feels?

   _____

Listening

🔊 Track 03

A NEW APARTMENT

Listen to the audio. Answer the questions.

COMPREHENSION

1. Who has a new apartment? _____

2. What floor is his apartment on? _____

3. How many boxes are not unpacked? _____

4. What do they plan to do? _____

5. What is Martin going to bring? _____

6. What is Dave's address? _____ O'Connor, Apt. _____

7. What is his new phone number? _____

8. What time is it now? _____

9. When does Martin expect to arrive? _____

10. Is Martin going to drive or take the bus? _____

Writing

Answer the following questions to write a short composition about yourself.

- What is your name?
- Where are you from?
- How old are you? When is your birthday?
- Do you have any brothers or sisters? How many?
- When do you usually get up in the morning?
- When do you come to school every day?
- When do you go home after your classes?
- How much time do you spend every day doing your homework?
- At what time do you usually go to sleep?
- Are there any activities you like to do on the weekend?

CHAPTER REVIEW

Summary

- Each word is a part of speech and has a specific function or use. Understanding how the parts of speech work together helps you create and use correct sentences more easily.

- Numbers give specific information about the time of day; personal information, such as dates and ages; and the quantity or costs of things.

- There are two ways to express the time: traditional and digital. Use the preposition *at* with a specific time and use *in* with a period of time, except with *night*.

- English has two kinds of nouns: countable and non-countable. Countable nouns have plural forms. Non-countable nouns are always singular.
- There are spelling rules for writing the plural forms. We add -s or -es to most nouns. Check the rules for words ending in y, o, f, fe, s, sh, ch, x, or z.
- Some nouns, like *sheep*, do not have a plural form.
- There are also some irregular plural nouns.
- We use the words *much* and *many* to show quantity with non-countable and countable nouns, respectively.
- The articles introduce nouns. Nouns can be indefinite (*a, an, some*), definite (*the, some*), or general (no article). We use *a* and *an* only with singular, countable nouns; we use *the* and *some* with countable and non-countable nouns.
- The structure *there + be* introduces information. *There is* introduces singular and non-countable nouns; *there are* introduces plural nouns.

EXERCISE 1

Fill in the blanks with the times you do the following things. Write the time in words and ⟨circle⟩ *at* or *in* to complete your answers.

Every day, I get up (⟨at⟩ / in) <u>six thirty (half past six)</u> (time) ₁ (at / in) the morning. I take a shower and get dressed by ₂ _____ (time). I usually leave for school (at / in) ₃ _____ (time). My class starts (at / in) ₄ _____ (time). I have lunch (at / in) ₅ _____ (time). ₆ (At / In) the afternoon, I go to class and study. I go home (at / in) ₇ _____ (time). I eat supper (at / in) ₈ _____ (time). I watch TV for a little while ₉ (at / in) the evening. I usually go to bed (at / in) ₁₀ _____ (time). Sometimes, I stay up late ₁₁ (at / in) night to study or to phone my friends.

EXERCISE 2

There are five plural noun errors in the following paragraph. Find and correct them.

There are so many activitys for people of all ages to do in the city. There are restaurantes, movies, and theatres. Everyone enjoys the parks too. I like to take a walk in the park on Sundays. I watch parent playing with their childrens or other people throwing Frisbees for their dogs. If it rains, I often go to the library to read books about the local history. It's fun to learn more informations about the place where you live.

EXERCISE 3

Fill in the blanks with *much, many, a little,* or *a few*.

1. How _____ time do we have before supper is ready? I just need

   _____ minutes to finish this exercise. The teacher gave us so

   _____ exercises to do.

2. We're having spaghetti and a salad. How _____ pasta would you

   like? Do you want a lot or just _____ sauce?

EXERCISE 4

There are five article errors in the following paragraph. Find and correct them.

The Mexico is great! I enjoy shopping when I'm on the holidays. I want to buy a dress. A blue one is nice, but it's the wrong size. I want to ask for a help, but I don't know how to say the words in Spanish. Do you think the clerk speaks the English?

EXERCISE 5

Write the correct choice in the blank to complete each sentence.

1. _____ there any good restaurants in your neighbourhood? (**Is / Are**)

2. There _____ a lot of homework to do for this course. (**is / are**)

3. The movie starts at 9:00. There _____ much time to get there. (**isn't / aren't**)

4. There _____ children playing in the park today. (**is / are**)

5. _____ there any butter in the fridge? (**Is / Are**)

Personal Pronouns, Demonstratives, the Imperative, and Prepositions

OVERVIEW

- Personal pronouns replace nouns and their modifiers.

- Demonstrative adjectives introduce nouns and show how near they are to the speaker; demonstrative pronouns replace the demonstrative adjectives and the nouns.

- The imperative gives instructions, commands, warnings, and advice.

- Prepositions tell us the relationship between people, things, or actions and place, time, direction, and origin. Prepositions of place tell us the relationship between people, things, or actions and place or location.

Warm-up

Work in pairs. Read the paragraph. First, <u>underline</u> all the verbs. (Circle) all the nouns and pronouns that appear in front of the verbs. Write the nouns and pronouns in the chart below. Write the verbs in the chart. There are four verbs that don't have a noun, a pronoun, or *to* in front of them. List them as imperative verbs. What do these verbs do?

Magdalena is one of our friends from school. She lives in a house a few blocks away from the college. Saturday is her daughter's fourth birthday. Magdalena wants to have a party. We plan to go to the party. Jerome wants to go too, but he doesn't know how to get to her house. There are two ways to get there.

Take the 97 bus from the shopping mall. Get off at Billings Avenue. Magdalena's house is three doors down from the corner at 64 Billings. Or, walk up Bartlow Street from the college. Turn right on Billings Avenue. Her house is not far.

Nouns	Pronouns	Verbs	Imperative Verbs

PERSONAL PRONOUNS

Personal pronouns replace nouns and their modifiers.

Warm-up

Work in pairs. Read the first paragraph. <u>Underline</u> all the nouns. Now read the second version of the paragraph. What is different? (Circle) the words that are in the places of the nouns you underlined.

George and his brother live in an apartment. The apartment is very small. George studies engineering at the college. His brother sometimes helps George with his homework.

They live in an apartment. It is very small. He studies engineering at the college. He sometimes helps him with it.

Formation

Subject Pronoun	Object Pronoun	Possessive Adjective (used with nouns)	Possessive Pronoun (replaces possessive adj. + noun)	Reflexive Pronoun
I	me	my (car)	mine	myself
you (sing.)	you	your (hat)	yours	yourself
he	him	his (cat)	his	himself
she	her	her (card)	hers	herself
it	it	its (meaning)	its	itself
we	us	our (house)	ours	ourselves
you (pl.)	you	your (friend)	yours	yourselves
they	them	their (family)	theirs	themselves

- *I* is always a capital letter.
- *You* has the same form in both singular and plural, except for the reflexive pronoun.
- *He*, *she*, and *it* are all the third-person singular; *he* is only for a male person, *she* is only for a female person, and *it* is for a thing or an animal.
- Notice that we create the reflexive pronouns from the possessive adjective form for all persons except *himself* and *themselves*. We often use the word *by* before the reflexive pronouns.

Subject pronouns control the action of the verb and appear in front of the verb in sentences.

John drives to work. → He drives to work.

Judy and her friends walk to school. → They walk to school.

Object pronouns replace the object of the verb or the object of a preposition.

Sarah teaches piano lessons on Saturday. → Sarah teaches them on Saturday.

Geraldo lives with his wife. → Geraldo lives with her.

Possessive adjectives are not pronouns. We use them with nouns to show possession.

Possessive pronouns replace possessive adjectives and the nouns.

Both possessive adjectives and possessive pronouns show the person (*I*, *you*, *they*, etc.), the number (singular or plural), and the gender (male or female) of the person or thing that has ownership. The noun that follows the possessive adjective or that the pronoun replaces does not influence the choice of possessive adjective or possessive pronoun.

> <u>John</u> drives <u>his car</u> to work.
>
> <u>Judy</u> and <u>her friends</u> walk to school.
>
> <u>We</u> have a small house. <u>Our house</u> is small. The small house is <u>ours</u>.
>
> <u>My books</u> are on the table. The books on the table are <u>mine</u>.

To show possession with nouns, add apostrophe + s ('s) to singular nouns and plural nouns that do not end in s. Add only the apostrophe (') to plural nouns ending in s.

The book belongs to Peter. It's Peter's book.

The children's toys are in the box.

The dogs' tails are wagging. They are happy.

EXERCISE 1

Fill in the blanks. Use the correct pronouns or possessive adjectives.

1. Fernando enjoys fixing things. When something breaks, he likes to fix it _____ (**herself / himself**).

2. My mother and _____ (**I / me**) like to go for a walk after dinner. Sometimes, my brother comes with _____ (**ours / us / we**).

3. The book on the table belongs to Maria. Please give it to _____ (**herself / her / hers**).

4. The brown shoes by the door are _____ (**me / my / mine**). _____ (**They / Their / Them**) are my favourite shoes.

5. The house on the corner belongs to us. It is _____ (**our / ours / ourselves**).

6. Mohammad and his cousin live in that apartment building. _____ (**They / Their / Theirs**) apartment is on the second floor.

7. Jennifer, you need to do your homework by _____ (**yours / yourself / yourselves**).

8. Sarah often plays soccer with _____ (**her / his / hers**) brothers.

9. Our cat has a favourite place to sleep. _____ (**He / She / It**) sleeps on _____ (**his / her / its**) pillow on the sofa.

10. The students study _____ (**our / their / them**) lessons by _____ (**ourselves / yourselves / themselves**).

EXERCISE 2

Replace the underlined words with pronouns or possessive adjectives.

<u>She</u>

Sofia shares an apartment with a friend. ~~Sofia~~ takes social work at the college. <u>Sofia's</u> roommate studies <u>social work</u> at the college too. <u>Sofia and Zara</u> take the bus to school every day. <u>Sofia's and Zara's</u> class schedules are the same. Sofia has a part-time job. <u>Sofia's</u> job is in the cafeteria. Zara often studies in the library and waits for <u>Sofia</u> to finish work. Then <u>Sofia and Zara</u> take the bus home. After supper, they do <u>Sofia's and Zara's</u> homework. Sometimes they do <u>homework</u> together and sometimes they do <u>homework</u> alone.

EXERCISE 3

🔊 Track 04

Look at the diagram of a family. Listen to the audio. Answer the questions.

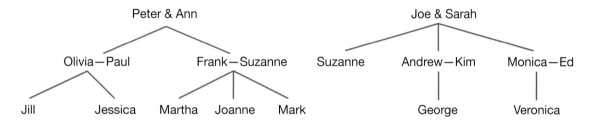

Family Members			
	Male	**Female**	**Group**
senior generation	grandfather	grandmother	grandparents
middle generation	father	mother	parents
young generation	son	daughter	children
young generation	brother	sister	siblings
young generation	grandson	granddaughter	grandchildren
middle generation	uncle	aunt	—
young generation	nephew	niece	cousins
middle generation	husband	wife	couple

COMPREHENSION

1. What is my name? Your name is _____.

2. What is my sister's name? Your sister's name is _____.

3. How many cousins do I have? You have _____ cousins.

4. What is the relationship between Jill and Jessica? Jill and Jessica are

    _____.

5. What is my relationship to George? George is your _____.

6. Who is Frank's wife? _____ is Frank's wife.

7. Who is Veronica's grandmother? _____ is her grandmother.

8. Who is Ann's grandson? _____ is her grandson.

9. Who is Olivia's husband? _____ is her husband.

10. What is my relationship to Paul? You are his _____.

DEMONSTRATIVE ADJECTIVES AND DEMONSTRATIVE PRONOUNS

Demonstrative adjectives introduce nouns and show how near they are to the speaker; demonstrative pronouns replace the demonstrative adjectives and the nouns.

Warm-up

Look at the picture. Read the description below.

Identify the people and things Andrea is describing in the picture. What do the words *this*, *that*, *these*, and *those* tell you about the location of the people and things in relation to where Andrea is? Are they near her or far from her?

My name is Andrea. I'm sitting on the bench in the picture. This spot is great for watching the people around me. That man is playing the guitar. Those children are playing with a ball. These birds want me to feed them. That family is having a picnic.

Formation

Near		Far	
Adjectives	**Pronouns**	**Adjectives**	**Pronouns**
This book is new.	**This** is new.	**That book** is brown.	**That** is brown.
These books are mine.	**These** are mine.	**Those books** are not mine.	**Those** are not mine

EXERCISE 4

Fill in the blanks. Use the correct demonstrative adjectives or pronouns to complete the sentences.

Are <u>those</u> your keys on the table by the door?

1. Look over there! What are _____ people doing?

2. I don't really like the shirt on the rack over there. I prefer _____ shirt.

3. Wow! _____ pizza is fantastic! Is it from Guillermo's Pizzeria?

4. There's a weird light in the park. What is _____?

5. Over there are the books you want. _____ are mine right here.

EXERCISE 5

There are six demonstrative adjectives or pronouns in the following paragraph. <u>Underline</u> them. Three are incorrect; correct them.

My grandparents have so many things packed away in this storage room. Look at these old boxes under all that stuff in the corner. Here is a book of old photos in that one. That box has a bunch of old toys. I wonder if these doll furniture is my mother's.

🔆 COMMUNICATIVE ACTIVITY 1

What Is This?

Work in small groups. Place a number of personal items, such as pens, books, cellphones, keys, and so on, on the desk. Together, write sentences using *this* and *these* that identify the objects on the desk. Then write sentences using *that* and *those* that identify the objects on another group's desk. Take turns reading the sentences out loud.

This is Frank's cellphone.

These keys are mine.

THE IMPERATIVE

The imperative gives instructions, commands, warnings, and advice.

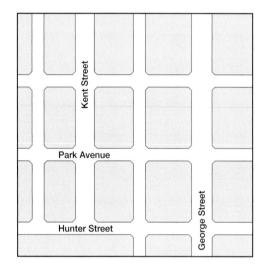

Warm-up

🔊 Track 05

Listen to the audio. Work in pairs, and trace the directions you hear on the map below. Try to include the landmarks (church, bank, and so on) mentioned in the telephone conversation. Compare your results with other pairs' results.

Formation

We use the imperative to give instructions, commands, and warnings. To form the imperative, use the base form of the verb for all verbs. There are no endings and no agreements, and nothing is irregular.

	Positive (base form of verb)	Negative (*do not* / *don't* + base form of verb)
Be	Be on time for class.	Don't be late for class.
Stay	Stay at home when you are sick.	Don't stay up late every night.
Sit	Sit down please.	Don't sit there.
Go	Go straight down this street.	Don't go to the store today.
Eat	Eat your vegetables.	Don't eat my lunch.

To make a suggestion for the first-person plural (*we*), use *let's* + the base form of the verb. *Let's* is the contracted form of *let us*.

	Positive (*let's* + base form of verb)	Negative (*let's* + *not* + base form of verb)
Be	Let's be on time for class.	Let's not be late for class.

Do	Let's do the dishes now.	Let's not do the dishes now.
Sit	Let's sit beside those guys.	Let's not sit beside those guys.
Go	Let's go to the movies tonight.	Let's not go to the movies tonight.
Eat	Let's eat pizza tonight.	Let's not eat pizza tonight.

EXERCISE 6

Change each of the following sentences into the imperative.

You need to bring your books to class. → Bring your books to class.

1. You need to take the number 18 bus to go to the grocery store.

   _____.

2. It's not a good idea to sit on that bench. It is wet from the rain.

   _____.

3. You need to be at work by 5:30.

   _____.

4. You need to practise your lessons.

   _____.

5. It's not a good idea to talk to strangers.

   _____.

EXERCISE 7

There are five imperative errors in the recipe. Find and correct them.

Scrambled Eggs

Heat the frying pan over medium heat. Cracks three eggs into a bowl. Add a little milk (five to ten millilitres). Season the eggs with some salt and pepper. Adds some herbs, such as marjoram or thyme, if desired. Beat the mixture with a whisk. Melts a tablespoon of butter in the frying pan. Pour the eggs into the pan. Once the eggs start to cook, turns the heat to medium low. Turn the eggs over in portions until cooked. Enjoys.

Giving Directions

Work in small groups. Take turns telling the others how to get from the school to the nearest bank, corner store, or grocery store. Use a local map to help you with the street names.

PREPOSITIONS OF PLACE

Prepositions of place tell us the relationship between people, things, or actions and place or location.

Warm-up

Work in pairs. Try to identify the prepositions of place—the words that introduce a location—in the paragraph. Underline them. Compare your answers with other pairs' answers.

I live in a nice neighbourhood. I live at 95 Park Avenue in apartment 1A on the first floor. My friend Miguel lives on the floor above me in apartment 2C. The laundry room is below my apartment, in the basement. There is a parking lot behind the building. My friend parks his car there. When I have visitors, they can park on the street. There is a convenience store across the street from my apartment building. Beside the store is a small park with lots of trees and a playground for the children in the neighbourhood. In front of the store is the bus stop. It's a great place to live.

Formation

Prepositions introduce nouns and their modifiers. Prepositions of place give information about the location of nouns and their relationship to other nouns. There are no rules for prepositions. You need to learn their meanings.

Common Prepositions of Place		
in front of	at	above
behind	on	below
beside	in	over
across from		under

In front of and *across from* can sometimes be synonyms but not always.

The teacher stands in front of the class. (not *across from*)

The park is across the street from my house. The park is in front of my house.

At, *on*, and *in* have two uses with location.

He sits at his desk. (his position) He lives at 151 Lakeside Avenue. (very specific location)

The book is on the desk. (its position) He lives on Lakeside Avenue. (larger location)

Your book is in the kitchen. (location in an area) He lives in Calgary. (large general location)

At is used with certain expression: *at home*, *at work*, *at school*.

Above and *over* are synonyms; *below* and *under* are synonyms.

EXERCISE 8

Look at the picture. Fill in the blanks with the best prepositions from the list in the Formation box. Some prepositions are used more than once.

There are three rows of desks $_1$ _____ the classroom. Melissa is sitting $_2$ _____ her desk. Her desk is the first in the row of desks $_3$ _____ the windows. Eugene is sitting $_4$ _____ Melissa in the same row of desks. The teacher is standing $_5$ _____ all the students $_6$ _____ his desk. He has a pointer $_7$ _____ his hand. He is pointing $_8$ _____ the exercise $_9$ _____ the blackboard. There is a clock $_{10}$ _____ the blackboard. There is a map on the wall $_{11}$ _____ the blackboard. $_{12}$ _____ the map, there is a desk. The desk has some books $_{13}$ _____ it, and there is a pile of magazines $_{14}$ _____ the desk.

BRINGING IT ALL TOGETHER

 ## COMMUNICATIVE ACTIVITY 3

How Do You . . . ?

Write instructions using the imperative for a simple activity. Try to use sequence markers, such as first, second, then, next, and so on. Here are some suggestions:

- how to make your favourite meal
- how to change a tire or the oil in a car
- how to create a particular kind of document on the computer
- how to replace a light fixture
- how to play a particular card game or sport

 ## COMMUNICATIVE ACTIVITY 4

Mini Oral Presentation

Work in small groups. Present your instructions from Communicative Activity 3 to your group. Ask questions about the other activities being presented.

COMMUNICATIVE ACTIVITY 5

People, Places, and Things

Work in pairs. Compete with your partner to write as many short sentences as possible about things or people in the classroom. Use *there is* or *there are* to begin the sentences, and use prepositions to give the location of the things. Give yourselves two to three minutes. The person with the most sentences wins. Compare your sentences to see how many are about different things.

Reading

Read the passage and answer the questions that follow.

> ### DIY
>
> DIY is an acronym or short form for Do it Yourself. The term means that people create, <u>renovate</u>, or repair all kinds of things without the direct help of a professional. Some people do DIY projects to save money. <u>Hiring</u> a professional to fix your toilet, for example, is often expensive. Other people enjoy the creative <u>aspect</u> of DIY. Completing a DIY project gives them a good feeling of success and accomplishment.

Doing it yourself is a very popular <u>trend</u> these days. DIY activities include everything from home improvement projects to arts and crafts to cooking to recording music and more. People complete or try to complete their projects by themselves without direct professional help. However, they very often <u>rely on</u> information from professionals to be able to do their projects. Many professionals and amateurs make a lot of money from sharing their <u>expertise</u>. There are thousands of "How to" books and magazines to help with DIY projects. There is at least one television channel on do-it-yourself topics. Many other television broadcasters have their own DIY programs as well. The Internet is also <u>loaded</u> with DIY sites.

There is a lot of information available for anyone who wants to complete a project by himself or herself. However, with so much information available, it is sometimes difficult to know if a source of information is good or not. Sometimes people who call themselves experts are not really experts at all. Always check more than one <u>source</u>, and compare the instructions and information. So, do it yourself. Good luck.

COMPREHENSION

Answer the following questions. Use complete sentences.

1. What does DIY mean?

   _____

2. Give two reasons that people do DIY projects.

   _____

3. Name three kinds of DIY activities.

   _____

4. Name three sources of information for DIY projects.

   _____

5. What advice does the writer give to help make sure the sources of information are good or reliable?

   _____

ANALYZING THE READING PASSAGE

Read the passage again and underline all personal pronouns (15) with a <u>single line</u>. Underline all the possessive adjectives (5) a <u>double line</u>. Circle the imperatives (3).

DISCUSSION

What is your opinion on do-it-yourself projects? Do you do any DIY projects? Give some examples of your projects.

Listening

🔊 Track 06

BEFORE THE CANOE TRIP

Listen to the audio.

COMPREHENSION

Answer the following questions. Write complete sentences.

1. Where are the friends going on Friday?

   _____

2. How many life jackets do they have?

   _____

3. They have two lighters. What else do they have?

   _____

4. What do they have lots of that is very important?

   _____

5. What do they need to buy tomorrow?

   _____

6. At what time do they agree to leave on Friday morning?

   _____

7. Why does one of the men call his friend crazy?

   _____

Writing

Write a short composition (maximum 150 words) about your usual leisure activities with family or friends on weekends or on holidays.
   Here are some questions to guide your writing:

- Do you have picnics in the park with family or friends?
- Do you get together with friends to play music, cards, or sports?
- When you take a vacation, do you travel, visit family, go camping, or do something else?

CHAPTER REVIEW

Summary

- Pronouns replace nouns and their modifiers.

- Demonstrative adjectives introduce nouns and show how near they are to the speaker; demonstrative pronouns replace the demonstrative adjectives and the nouns.

- Use the imperative to give instructions, commands, warnings, and advice.

- Prepositions of place tell us the relationship between people, things, or actions and place or location.

EXERCISE 1

Unscramble the following words and make them into sentences.

we eat / to the park / Let's / after / go → Let's go to the park after we eat.

1. does / with her friends / Marlena / her homework

   _____

2. at home / I / in the evening / study _____

3. are mine / belong to Philip / , but these / Those books

   _____

4. is / about pronouns / tomorrow / Our test

   _____

5. at / left / the next corner / Turn _____

EXERCISE 2

Circle the letter of the correct pronoun to complete the sentences.

1. The students listen to _____ teacher.   a) his   b) theirs   c) their

2. Allija tries to fix her computer by _____.   a) her   b) herself   c) itself

3. Stephan has lunch with _____ wife on Fridays.   a) her   b) his   c) him

4. Manolo and _____ need to study for our test.   a) I   b) me   c) us

5. Those aren't your keys. They are _____.   a) my   b) hers   c) our

EXERCISE 3

Fill in the blanks with the missing pronouns.

My boyfriend Jorge has a large family. **His** grandparents have six children. Now
1 _____ have twenty-one grandchildren and three great-grandchildren.
That's just on 2 _____ mother's side of the family. Jorge's father has
three brothers and two sisters, and 3 _____ all have children. In fact,
4 _____ children are all between the ages of seventeen and twenty. Jorge
says all the cousins have great fun when his parents have a big family gathering for
all of 5 _____ once a year.

EXERCISE 4

There are five errors with personal pronouns or the demonstrative adjectives (*this*, *that*,
these, and *those*) in the following paragraph. Correct them.

I enjoy watching people. For example, this young girl over there looks like she is
talking to himself. She is really talking on the phone. There is a couple sitting on
those park bench. The man looks nervous. Perhaps the couple is on a first date. These
kids over there are playing with a ball. Oops! The ball is now in that pond. There are
some teenagers walking near the pond. One of they is getting the ball out of the water.

EXERCISE 5

Change the following instructions into the imperative.

It's a good idea to test the temperature of the water. → Test the temperature of the water.

To get to the museum, you need to go straight down this street. You need to turn
right onto First Avenue. Then you need to walk for two blocks. You turn left on
Frank Street. You need to walk to the end. The museum is right in front of you.

_____

_____

_____

_____

_____

Simple Present

OVERVIEW

We use the simple present verb tense to express facts and generalizations, as well as actions that happen on a regular basis. Such actions include routines, habits, and daily activities.

Use	Form	Keywords	Example Sentences
facts or generalizations	most verbs: I / you / we / they + **verb** she / he / it + **verb** + s / es	every day / Monday / Tuesday every weekend every year every summer every vacation / holiday always usually often sometimes rarely never	I **read** books. The earth **circles** the sun. I **go** on vacation every summer. She **works** every weekend. They usually **leave** at five o'clock.
routines habits daily activities	verb *be*: I **am** she / he / it **is** you / we / they **are**		I **am** always honest. You **are** a student. It **is** difficult.
	verb *have*: I / you / we / they **have** she / he / it **has**	once a day / week / year twice per day / week / year number of times per day / week / year	I **have** a dessert once a week. We **have** a house. He **has** a car.

Warm-up

Read the following passage, and <u>underline</u> the verbs in the simple present tense.

> I have a sister. Her name is Izabela. She is older than I am. I live in Ottawa, but she lives in Toronto. She works as a sales representative. She likes her job. She has a son. He is 14 years old. He plays drums, takes martial arts classes, and studies hard. He also likes to play video games. My sister and I often call each other. We usually talk about our family. I really love my sister. Do you have any brothers or sisters? Are you in contact with them?

Write the verbs from the passage for the following subjects:

I, we: _____

she, he: _____

you: _____

Can you see any patterns? _____

SIMPLE PRESENT—REGULAR VERBS

All verbs except *be* have two forms in the simple present. For *I*, *you*, *we*, and *they*, use the base form of the verb. For *he*, *she*, and *it*, add *-s* or *-es*.

Warm-up

Work in pairs. Read the following conversations out loud.

Conversation 1
Partner A: What time do you **usually** wake up?
Partner B: I **usually** wake up at seven in the morning.

Conversation 2
Partner A: Do you work?
Partner B: No, I go to college. I study in a hairdressing program.
Partner A: Do you like it?
Partner B: I love it!

Conversation 3

Partner A: What do you **usually** do during summer?

Partner B: I **always** visit my family in Vancouver for the first two weeks of summer. After, I come back to Ottawa, and I **usually** get a summer job.

Partner A: Do you **sometimes** spend some time with your friends?

Partner B: Yes, I see them on weekends. We **often** rent a movie or go out.

Read the warm-up conversations again. Notice the placement of the adverbs.

Formation

Positive	Negative	Question
Subject + Verb (+ object / complement)	Subject + Auxiliary + Negative + Verb (+ object / complement)	Auxiliary + Subject + Verb (+ object / complement)
I **wake** up at 7:00 AM every day.	I **do not wake** up at 7:00 AM every day.	**Do** you **wake** up at 7:00 AM every day?
You **watch** TV in the evening.	You **do not watch** TV in the evening.	**Do** you **watch** TV in the evening?
He **likes** Honda cars.	He **does not like** Honda cars.	**Does** he **like** Honda cars?
She **reads** a lot.	She **does not read** a lot.	**Does** she **read** a lot?
It **costs** five dollars.	It **does not cost** five dollars.	**Does** it **cost** five dollars?
We **travel** to Yukon every summer.	We **do not travel** to Yukon every summer.	**Do** we **travel** to Yukon every summer?
They **work** on weekends.	They **do not work** on weekends.	**Do** they **work** on weekends?

Note: For a detailed explanation of how to form and use questions and negatives, refer to Chapter 11.

QUESTION WORDS FOR WH- QUESTIONS

Question words ask about a specific piece of information in a sentence. We use them when making wh- questions.

The wh- question formation is the same as for yes / no questions. We just put in a question word before we add the rest of the question.

Question Word	Use	Example Sentences	Wh- Question
			Question Word +Auxiliary + Subject + Verb (+ object / complement)
who	only people	Alex loves **Milo**.	**Who** does Alex love?
what	things or actions	They build **houses**. He **hangs out with his friends** every Friday.	**What** do they build? **What** does he do every Friday?
where	places	She works at **McDonald's**.	**Where** does she work?
when	time	My class starts **at 9:00**.	**When** does your class start?
why	reasons	He studies a lot **because he wants good grades**. I paint every weekend **to relax**.	**Why** does he study a lot? **Why** do you paint every weekend?
how	manner or degree	She goes to work **by bus**. I feel **great**!	**How** does she go to work? **How** do you feel?
how much / how many	quantity	It costs **10 dollars**. We have **two** cats.	**How much** does it cost? **How many** cats do you have?
how far	distance	I live **50 kilometres** from here.	**How far** do you live from here?
how long	duration	It usually takes us **half a day** to clean our house.	**How long** does it usually take us to clean our house?
how often	frequency	They meet **once** a week.	**How often** do they meet?

EXERCISE 1

Fill in the blanks with the correct question words. Each question word needs to correspond with the portion of the sentence **in bold** and underlined.

I use reusable bags <u>because I want to be environmentally friendly</u>.

<u>Why</u> do you use reusable bags?

1. **<u>A lot of</u>** people try to carpool to work these days.

   _____ people try to carpool to work these days?

2. Common recyclable materials include **glass, metal, plastic, and paper**.

   _____ do recyclable materials include?

3. **My friend** reuses clean yogourt containers to plant flower seeds.

   _____ reuses clean yogourt containers to plant flower seeds?

4. We help to clean up a local park **every spring**.

   _____ do we help to clean up a local park?

5. My son learns **at school and at home** that it is important to care about our environment.

   _____ does my son learn that it is important to care about our environment?

FREQUENCY ADVERBS

In the simple present, we often use frequency adverbs. These adverbs tell us how often an action takes place.

0%	never	I **never** lie.
	rarely/seldom	My school volleyball team **rarely** loses any games.
	occasionally	She **occasionally** eats red meat.
	sometimes	They **sometimes** do silly things.
	generally	We **generally** buy our groceries at a local store.
	often	You **often** forget what I tell you.
	usually	The bus **usually** comes on time.
100%	always	Evgeny **always** works on Saturdays.

With regular verbs, we place adverbs before the verb.

EXERCISE 2

Unscramble the following words and make them into sentences or questions.

snows / in / It / Canada → It snows in Canada.

1. with / She / lives / her parents

   _____.

2. don't / buy / They / any junk food / usually

   _____.

3. your class / at eight o'clock / always / Does / start

   _____?

4. England /come / My father / doesn't / from

   _____.

5. you / ride / Do / on a motorcycle?

   _____?

SPELLING RULES FOR VERBS IN THE THIRD-PERSON SINGULAR

Rules	Examples	
Add -s for most verbs	work: works speak: speaks	travel → travels
Add -es for verbs that end in *ch*, *s*, *sh*, *x*, or *z*.	watch: watches pass: passes wash: washes	fix → fixes buzz: buzzes
Add -es for verbs that end in a single vowel. Add -s for verbs that end in two vowels.	go: goes tattoo: tattoos	do → does
Change the *y* to *i* and add -es when the base form ends in a consonant and *y*. Do not change the *y* when the verb ends in a vowel and *y*. Add only an -s.	study: studies pay: pays	carry → carries

For the pronunciation rules for the -s endings, see page 12 in Chapter 1.

EXERCISE 3

Write the correct spelling of the following verbs in the third-person singular.

1. look _____
2. want _____
3. brush _____
4. play _____
5. hope _____
6. hurry _____
7. try _____
8. write _____

9. relax _____
10. enjoy _____
11. travel _____
12. match _____
13. go _____
14. stay _____
15. arrive _____

EXERCISE 4

Answer each question with a complete sentence. Look at the examples to help you.

Do you speak other languages? Yes, I speak other languages.

Does she do her homework every night? No, she doesn't do her homework every night.

1. Do Simon and Derek know how to cook?

   No, _____

2. Does your daughter like to read?

   Yes, _____

3. Do dogs bark?

   Yes, _____

4. Do you have a pet?

   No, _____

5. Does he play football?

   No, _____

COMMUNICATIVE ACTIVITY 1

Find the Order

Work in pairs or in small groups. Put the following sentences in sequence to make them into a story. Write a number (1–8) next to each sentence to show the order. (Hint: The story starts in the morning.)

_____ I usually eat my lunch at noon.

_____ After dinner, I help my daughter with her homework.

_____ I have breakfast before I leave for work.

_____ I often go to bed at 11 PM.

_____ I get up at seven o'clock in the morning.

_____ In the evening, I sometimes call my friends.

_____ When I come back from work, I cook dinner for my family.

_____ I start work at nine o'clock.

SIMPLE PRESENT—THE VERB *BE*

The verb *be* is irregular in the simple present.

Warm-up

Tell your partner about yourself. You can include some information from the chart below.

Category	Your Information
age	(_____ years old)
nationality	(for example, Canadian, Mexican)
marital / family status	(for example, single, married, a mother / a father)
personality	(for example, friendly, shy, hard-working, ambitious)
profession	(for example, a student, a nurse, an engineer, a computer technician)

Now, your partner will tell you about himself or herself. Write in any information he or she gives you.

Category	Partner's Information
age	
nationality	
marital / family status	
personality	
profession	

Formation

Positive	Negative	Question	Wh- Question
Subject + Verb + Complement	Subject + Verb + Negative + Complement	Verb + Subject + Complement	Question Word + Verb + Subject (+ complement)
I **am** Jeanne's sister.	I **am not** Jeanne's sister.	**Are** you Jeanne's sister?	**Who** are you?

Positive	Negative	Question	Wh- Question
You **are** 25 years old.	You **are not** 25 years old.	**Are** you 25 years old?	**How old** are you?
He **is** sad.	He **is not** sad.	**Is** he sad?	**Why** is he sad?
She **is** Canadian.	She **is not** Canadian.	**Is** she Canadian?	**What nationality** is she?
It **is** 10 dollars.	It **is not** 10 dollars.	**Is** it 10 dollars?	**How much** is it?
We **are** from Ottawa.	We **are not** from Ottawa.	**Are** we from Ottawa?	**Where** are we from?
They **are** on vacation.	They **are not** on vacation.	**Are** they on vacation?	**Where** are they?

- Remember, the verb *be* does not need an auxiliary verb in negatives or questions.
- Adverb placement: Adverbs are placed after the verb *be*.

  He is <u>never</u> late for work.

EXERCISE 5

Fill in the blanks with the correct form of the verb *be* in the simple present tense.

We <u>are</u> from Manitoba.

1. She _____ a doctor.

2. _____ it cold today?

3. They _____ not afraid of the dark.

4. His name _____ Steve.

5. _____ you at home?

EXERCISE 6

Answer each question with a complete sentence.

Is it beautiful?   **Yes, it is beautiful.**

1. Are you an English student? Yes, _____

2. Is she a teacher? Yes, _____

3. Is he from Spain? No, _____

4. Are you and your classmates at school? Yes, _____

5. Is this room blue? No, _____

EXERCISE 7

Change each of the following sentences into a yes / no question.

I am happy. → **Are you happy?**

1. Tom and Chris are friends.

   _____?

2. We are at work.

   _____?

3. This book is interesting.

   _____?

4. She is absent.

   _____?

5. You are very smart.

   _____?

COMMUNICATIVE ACTIVITY 2

Mini Oral Presentation

Based on the information from the warm-up activity in Simple Present—The Verb *Be* (on pages 46–47), prepare a short oral report about your partner. You can ask him or her additional questions. Then, present your report to the whole class. Your classmates can ask you or your partner more questions.

SIMPLE PRESENT—THE VERB *HAVE*

The verb *have* has two forms in the simple present but one form is irregular.

Warm-up

FIND SOMEONE WHO . . .

On a separate piece of paper, prepare some yes / no questions for your classmates. Use the five ideas on the next page to get you started.

Find someone who

- has many hobbies.
- has dreams every night.
- has a part-time job.
- has a doctor's appointment today.
- has a good memory.

Then ask some of your classmates the questions. If somebody answers "yes" to your question, record his or her name, and write the answers in complete sentences. Look at the example to help you.

Questions	Names + Answers
Do you have a laptop?	Sandra has a laptop.

Formation

Positive	Negative	Question	Wh- Question
Subject + Verb (+ object)	Subject + Auxiliary + Negative + Verb (+ object)	Auxiliary + Subject + Verb (+ object)	Question Word + Auxiliary + Subject + Verb (+ object)
I **have** two brothers.	I **do not have** two brothers.	**Do** you **have** two brothers?	**How many** brothers do you have?
You **have** a cold.	You **do not have** a cold.	**Do** you **have** a cold?	**Why** do you have a cold?
She **has** a parrot.	She **does not have** a parrot.	**Does** she **have** a parrot?	**What kind of** pet does she have?
He **has** brown eyes.	He **does not have** brown eyes.	**Does** he **have** brown eyes?	**What** eye colour does he have?
It **has** a sunroof.	It **does not have** a sunroof.	**Does** it **have** a sunroof?	**What** does it have?
We **have** some plans.	We **do not have** any plans.	**Do** we **have** any plans?	**What** plans do we have?
They **have** a cottage in Madawaska.	They **do not have** a cottage in Madawaska.	**Do** they **have** a cottage in Madawaska?	**Where** do they have a cottage?

EXERCISE 8

Fill in the blanks with the correct form of the verb *have* in the simple present tense.

You _____ (have) a dog. → You **have** a dog.

She _____ (have, negative) a cat. → She **does not have** a cat.

1. Carolina _____ (have) many talents.

2. He _____ (have, negative) any allergies.

3. (have, question) _____ they _____ any problems?

4. My daughter and I _____ (have) curly hair.

5. This hotel _____ (have) an indoor pool.

BRINGING IT ALL TOGETHER

 ## COMMUNICATIVE ACTIVITY 3

Partner Interview

Work with a partner. On a separate sheet of paper, make an interview chart like the one below. Write some yes / no questions to ask your partner. Ask about his or her daily habits or weekly routine. Look at the example to help you.

You	Your Partner
What time do you usually leave home every day?	I usually leave home at 8:00 AM.

COMMUNICATIVE ACTIVITY 4

Find Someone Who . . .

Prepare yes / no questions for your classmates. Use the information below. Then ask some of your classmates the questions. If somebody answers "yes" to your question, record his or her name, and write the answer in a complete sentence. Look at the example to help you.

Find someone who . . . lives in Ottawa.

Question: Do you live in Ottawa?   **Answer: Anne lives in Ottawa.**

Find someone who . . .

1. plays a musical instrument.

   Question: _____ Answer: _____

2. has a brother or a sister.

   Question: _____ Answer: _____

3. usually wakes up early in the morning.

   Question: _____ Answer: _____

4. likes chocolate.

   Question: _____ Answer: _____

5. drives to school every day.

   Question: _____ Answer: _____

 ## COMMUNICATIVE ACTIVITY 5

Surveys

Work in small groups. Your teacher will give your group a worksheet with one survey on an assigned topic. Each group member conducts a survey with at least one student from a different group. When you finish the surveys, meet with your group again to tally the responses and to prepare a short presentation of the results to the whole class.

 ## COMMUNICATIVE ACTIVITY 6

Game—What's the Profession?

Work in pairs or small groups. Think of a profession, but don't tell your partner or group what it is. Prepare three to four sentences about what a person working in this profession usually does. Your partner or group will try to guess what the profession is.

> **This person usually inspects vehicles. He or she often changes oil and replaces car brakes. In general, this person fixes cars. (Answer: a car mechanic)**

Reading

Read the passage and answer the questions that follow.

WEEKEND BREAKFAST WITH FAMILY

The weekend is usually filled with sports, play-dates, and errands, but it is also a great opportunity for the entire family to spend time together. A great way to do this is to start with a balanced family breakfast. A balanced breakfast at the beginning of the day is important. It often prepares you and your family for whatever your weekend has in store. Here are some helpful tips for a weekend family breakfast:

Participation
One of the best ways to make breakfast a family affair is to get everyone involved. Every family member has a task to do. A fun recipe to make on an <u>assembly line</u> is banana rollups. One family member spreads Nutella on a slice of whole grain pita, another member tops it off with sliced bananas, and the third rolls it up.

Family Traditions
A weekly family breakfast gives everyone something to <u>look forward to</u> and turns breakfast into a social activity <u>instead of</u> just a meal. It is a nice way to make it a family tradition and to spend valuable <u>quality time</u>.

<u>Extend</u> the Invitation
The weekend is the perfect occasion to spend time with other family members whom you do not usually see during the week. You can welcome everyone—grandparents, cousins, aunts, and uncles. This creates a stronger family tradition and leads to better habits.

Adapted from "Make Breakfast a Family Affair." *Ottawa Family Living Magazine*, www.ottawafamilyliving.com/make_breakfast_a_family_affair.

COMPREHENSION

Answer the questions. Use complete sentences.

1. What activities usually fill up the weekend?

   _____

2. Why is a balanced breakfast at the beginning of the day important?

   _____

3. How can each family member be involved in a weekend breakfast?

   _____

4. In what way is the family weekend breakfast a social activity?

   _____

5. Whom can you invite to such a breakfast?

   _____

ANALYZING THE READING PASSAGE

Read the passage again, and <u>underline</u> all the present tense verbs with a single line and all the adverbs with a <u>double line</u>.

DISCUSSION

1. Agree or disagree with this statement: "A weekend breakfast with family is a good idea." Explain your answer.

   _____

2. In your family, do you usually have breakfast together? What other activities do you do with your family members to spend time together?

   _____

Listening

🔊 Track 07

EARLY CLASSES = SLEEPY TEENS!

Listen to the audio. Answer the questions.

COMPREHENSION

Answer the following questions. Write complete sentences in the simple present tense.

1. Do American teenagers get enough sleep?

   _____

2. What time do many schools start their classes?

   _____

3. Who is Michael Breus?

   _____

4. How many hours of sleep do teenagers need per night?

   _____

5. What does Michael Breus say about sleepy teens?

   _____

6. What can schools do to resolve this problem?

   _____

Writing

Choose one of the topics below. Write a short composition (maximum 150 words) about the topic.

- What do you usually do during school breaks or winter or summer vacations?
- How do you usually celebrate your birthday or other family events?

CHAPTER REVIEW

Summary

- We use the simple present for facts, generalizations, and actions that take place on a regular basis.

- With the simple present tense, we use certain keywords or phrases, such as *every day*, *every summer*, or *twice a month*, as well as frequency adverbs, such as *always*, *often*, *sometimes*, and *never*.

- With all verbs except *be*, there are two forms in the simple present. For the pronouns *I*, *you*, *we*, and *they*, use the base form of the verb. For *he*, *she*, and *it*, add *-s* or *-es*.

- The verb *be* is irregular in the simple present and is different for every subject. It has three forms: *am* (*I am*), *are* (*you are*, *we are*, *they are*), and *is* (*he is*, *she is*, *it is*).

- The verb *have* is also irregular, and it has two forms: *have* (*I have*, *you have*, *we have*, *they have*) and *has* (*he has*, *she has*, *it has*).

EXERCISE 1

Change each of the following positive sentences into the negative. Review the formation charts in this chapter on pages 41, 46–47, and 49 if you need to. Look at the examples to help you.

You like chocolate.   Negative: You do not like chocolate.

She is a college student.   Negative: She is not a college student.

1. He has breakfast at 8:00 AM.

   _____

2. We usually go out on Fridays.

   _____

3. They are on vacation.

_____

4. My son calls me every weekend.

_____

5. I am a mother.

_____

EXERCISE 2

Change each of the following sentences into a yes / no question. Review the formation charts in this chapter on pages 41, 46–47, and 49 if you need to. Look at the examples to help you.

Anna lives by herself.   **Question: Does Anna live by herself?**

My friends are from Montreal.   **Question: Are my friends from Montreal?**

1. We travel every summer.

_____

2. My neighbours are very nice.

_____

3. She helps her grandmother every weekend.

_____

4. I have a toothache.

_____

5. He is always on time.

_____

EXERCISE 3

Change each of the following statements into a wh- question. The information you want to ask about is underlined and **in bold**. Review the wh- question words on page 42, and the formation charts in this chapter on pages 41, 46–47, and 49 if you need to. Look at the example to help you.

Canadians celebrate Canada Day on July 1st.

Question: What do Canadians celebrate on July 1st?

1. People use computers **all over the world**.

_____

2. Social people like **to spend time with others**.

    _____

3. Irene and I usually leave for work **at 9:00 AM**.

    _____

4. Camille and Felix take **skating lessons** on Saturday.

    _____

5. Robert has **nine grandchildren**.

    _____

EXERCISE 4

There are five simple present verb tense errors in the following passage. Find and correct them.

Every Sunday, my parents invites my family for dinner at their house. We usually

go there at three o'clock. My daughter and I often helps my mom with the dinner

preparation. My husband like to talk with my father. We eat dinner at five o'clock.

After, we sit in the living room and we all have coffee while our daughter haves

some ice cream. My parents and my family is always happy to spend time with one

another.

EXERCISE 5

Underline the correct choice to complete each sentence.

1. They don't _____ meat. (**eat / eats**)

2. _____ Henry and you know each other? (**Does / Do**)

3. She _____ late for school. (**is sometimes / sometimes is**)

4. Hannah and Jade _____ on a vacation in July. (**go often / often go**)

5. Ottawa _____ the capital of Canada. (**are / is**)

Present Progressive

OVERVIEW

We use the present progressive verb tense to express actions that are happening right now, temporary actions, actions in progress, and future arrangements.

Use	Form	Keywords	Example Sentences
right now		now right now at the moment	I **am reading** a book now. You **are jogging** right now. They **are eating** at the moment.
temporary actions	*am / is / are* + base form of a verb + *ing* (present participle)	currently temporarily for a week	She **is staying** with me for one week.
longer actions in progress		this week, month, year	He **is taking** an English course this semester.
future arrangements		tonight soon	We **are coming** back from Florida tonight.

PRESENT PROGRESSIVE— REGULAR VERBS

For regular verbs, we form the present progressive by combining the present tense of *be* with the present participle (or *-ing* form) of the verb.

Warm-up

Work in pairs. Read the following conversations out loud.

CONVERSATION 1

Partner A: Hi, John! This is Sam. What are you doing?
Partner B: Hi, Sam. I am studying.
Partner A: Are you studying for our math exam this Friday?
Partner B: No, I'm not. I am studying for my English class.

CONVERSATION 2

Partner A: Excuse me?
Partner B: Yes, how can I help you?
Partner A: I am looking for the Atlantic salmon that is on sale. Do you have any?
Partner B: Sorry. We don't have any in stock right now, but we are getting more this afternoon. Come back after five o'clock or so.
Partner A: Thank you.

Read the warm-up conversations again. Try to guess what the following verbs have in common: *doing, studying, looking, getting.*

Formation

Positive	Negative	Question	Wh- Question
Subject + *be* + Verb *-ing* (+ object / complement)	Subject + *be* + Negative + Verb *-ing* (+ object / complement)	*Be* + Subject + Verb *-ing* (+ object / complement)	Question Word + *be* + Subject + Verb *-ing* (+ object / complement)
I **am** talk**ing** now.	I **am not** talk**ing** now.	**Are** you talk**ing** now?	**What** are you do**ing** now?
You **are** study**ing** English this semester.	You **are not** study**ing** English this semester.	**Are** you study**ing** English this semester?	**Why** are you study**ing** English this semester?

Positive	Negative	Question	Wh- Question
He **is** fix**ing** his car right now.	He **is not** fix**ing** his car right now.	**Is** he fix**ing** his car right now?	**What** is he fix**ing** right now?
She **is** paint**ing** her room.	She **is not** paint**ing** her room.	**Is** she paint**ing** her room?	**Whose** room is she paint**ing**?
It **is** rain**ing**.	It **is not** rain**ing**.	**Is** it rain**ing**?	**Where** is it rain**ing**?
We **are** watch**ing** TV.	We **are not** watch**ing** TV.	**Are** we watch**ing** TV?	**What** are we watch**ing**?
They **are** sleep**ing**.	They **are not** sleep**ing**.	**Are** they sleep**ing**?	**Where** are they sleep**ing**?

Note: For a detailed explanation of how to form and use questions and negatives, refer to Chapter 11.

SPELLING RULES FOR VERBS WITH -*ING* ENDING

Rule	Examples	
For most verbs, add -*ing* to the base form of the verb.	work → working snow → snowing	drink → drinking do → doing
If a verb ends in a silent *e*, drop the final *e* and add -*ing*.	write → writing smile → smiling	arrive → arriving skate → skating
In a one-syllable word that ends in a consonant-vowel-consonant (CVC) combination, double the last consonant before adding -*ing*. Do not double the last consonant in a word that ends in *w*, *x*, or *y*.	clap → clapping jog → jogging sit → sitting fix → fixing	
In words of two or more syllables that end in a consonant-vowel-consonant combination, double the last consonant only if the last syllable is stressed. If the last syllable is not stressed, just add -*ing*.	begin → beginning refer → referring happen → happening	
If a verb ends in *ie*, change the *ie* to *y* before adding -*ing*.	tie → tying lie → lying	

EXERCISE 1

Unscramble the following words and make them into sentences or questions.

playing / We / are / soccer → **We are playing soccer.**

1. looking at / Rose / is / her photos

   _____.

2. not / Christie and Jim / flying to Vancouver / are / now

   _____.

3. a shower / taking / Is / David

   _____?

4. is / the floor / Anne-Marie / cleaning

   _____.

5. you / Are / your baby / feeding

   _____?

EXERCISE 2

Write the correct spelling of the following verbs with an *-ing* ending.

chew → **chewing**

1. talk   _____
2. whistle   _____
3. discuss   _____
4. cook   _____
5. go   _____
6. run   _____
7. pay   _____
8. whisper   _____

9. bike   _____
10. teach   _____
11. laugh   _____
12. die   _____
13. sneeze   _____
14. sweep   _____
15. hop   _____

✵ COMMUNICATIVE ACTIVITY 1

Spelling Bee

Work in teams. Taking turns, one team chooses a verb from the Base Form column of the chart in Appendix A: Common Irregular Verbs. One member of another team spells the verb with an *-ing* ending. This can be done orally or in writing on the board. If the spelling is correct, that student's team scores a point. If not, then another team gets a chance to spell it correctly and steal the point instead.

PRESENT PROGRESSIVE VERSUS SIMPLE PRESENT

Remember, use the simple present for facts, habits, and actions that happen on a regular basis. Use the present progressive for the actions that are happening now. However, we cannot use certain verbs in the present progressive tense even if the action is right now. Instead, we use the simple present tense for them.

Warm-up

Read the passage and answer the question that follows.

> In this picture, you **see** a mother and her three children. They **are** at a grocery store. They **are buying** groceries for the entire week, so their shopping cart **is** full of groceries. Right now, the mother **is looking** at the label of a product, and she **is checking** its ingredients. The little boy **is sitting** in the shopping cart, and he **is holding** a juice carton. The older boy **is looking** at his mom. The girl **is looking** at the groceries, and she **is laughing**. It **seems** they **are having** fun at the store. I **think** they **like** to go shopping with their mom.

Look at the verbs **in bold**. What two verb tenses can you recognize?

NON-PROGRESSIVE VERBS

A non-progressive verb is a verb that we cannot use in the progressive verb tense.

	Non-progressive Verbs	Verbs That Can Be Either Regular or Non-progressive		Example Sentence
Senses		hear* feel* see*	smell* taste*	I hear someone at the door.
Possession	belong own	possess	have*		That book belongs to the teacher.

Continued

	Non-progressive Verbs		Verbs That Can Be Either Regular or Non-progressive		Example Sentence
Emotions	dislike hate like	love need prefer	care* want*		I love this shirt.
Thoughts	believe desire know	realize recognize understand	feel* forget* imagine*	mean* remember* think*	I know it's true.
Being	seem sound	resemble exist	appear* be* cost*	include* look* weigh*	The test seems difficult.

The verbs with an asterisk (*) have more than one meaning. When we use them in the progressive tense, their essential meanings change.

			Example Sentence	
	Verbs		**Non-progressive Verb Use**	**Progressive Verb Use**
Senses	hear* feel* see*	smell* taste*	I **hear** someone at the door. (the physical sense)	I don't hear anyone. You **are hearing** things. (not hearing, but imagining)
Possession	have*		I **have** a daughter. (possession)	I **am having** dinner now. (action of eating)
Emotions	care* want*		They **care** about us. (emotion)	She **is caring** for her mother. (action of providing care)
Thoughts	feel* forget* imagine*	mean* remember* think*	I **think** it's important. (thought or belief)	I **am thinking** about what to cook for dinner. (using thought to make a decision)
Being	appear* be* cost*	include* look* weigh*	She **weighs** 70 kilograms. (state or fact)	The nurse **is weighing** the newborn now. (action of finding out the weight)

EXERCISE 3

Fill in the blanks with the correct form of the verbs in the present progressive or simple present.

You _____ (wash) dishes now. → You <u>are washing</u> dishes now.

She _____ (like) flowers. → She <u>likes</u> flowers.

1. Right now, my boss ＿＿＿＿＿＿＿＿ (give) me instructions.

2. Samuel ＿＿＿＿＿＿＿＿ (want) to be a firefighter.

3. We ＿＿＿＿＿＿＿＿ (think, negative) it's a good idea.

4. I ＿＿＿＿＿＿＿＿ (know) the answer to this question.

5. Scott ＿＿＿＿＿＿＿＿ (clean) his motorcycle at the moment.

EXERCISE 4

Change each of the following sentences into a yes / no question.

I am cooking now. → Are you cooking now?

We cook every day. → Do you cook every day?

1. Annette is talking on the phone with her friend.

＿＿＿＿＿＿＿＿＿＿＿＿＿＿＿＿＿＿＿＿＿＿＿＿＿＿＿？

2. They work every day.

＿＿＿＿＿＿＿＿＿＿＿＿＿＿＿＿＿＿＿＿＿＿＿＿＿＿＿？

3. My mom calls me every weekend.

＿＿＿＿＿＿＿＿＿＿＿＿＿＿＿＿＿＿＿＿＿＿＿＿＿＿＿？

4. I am preparing lunch for my husband.

＿＿＿＿＿＿＿＿＿＿＿＿＿＿＿＿＿＿＿＿＿＿＿＿＿＿＿？

5. You take good photos.

＿＿＿＿＿＿＿＿＿＿＿＿＿＿＿＿＿＿＿＿＿＿＿＿＿＿＿？

⁘ COMMUNICATIVE ACTIVITY 2

What's in the Picture?

Work with a partner. Your teacher will give you each a picture from a magazine. Don't show your partner your picture. Describe the picture to your partner by using the present progressive and the simple present. Your partner will draw what he or she thinks your picture looks like. Then, your partner will describe his or her picture. Sketch it on a separate sheet of paper. You can ask each other additional questions. At the end of the activity, show your pictures to each other.

BRINGING IT ALL TOGETHER

 ## COMMUNICATIVE ACTIVITY 3

Game—What Am I Doing?

Work in two teams. Taking turns, a student from one team stands at the front of the classroom, where he or she receives a piece of paper with an action verb on it. The student mimes the action and his or her group has to guess what the student is doing. If they guess correctly, the team then has to make up a sentence that uses the verb in the present progressive. If they provide a correct sentence, they get a point. If the group can't give a correct response in 30 seconds, the other team gets a chance to make up a sentence and score a point.

 ## COMMUNICATIVE ACTIVITY 4

🔊 Track 08

What's That Noise?

Work in pairs. Listen to the audio in which people and animals are making noises. For each noise, use the following verbs to write a sentence in the present progressive. If you do not know the meaning of some verbs, ask your partner or together look up the words in a dictionary.

| knock | snore | laugh | bark | hum | cough |

1. Tom _____

2. Yuki and Makato _____

3. The dog _____

4. You _____

5. I _____

6. Richard _____

COMMUNICATIVE ACTIVITY 5

Game—What's Happening?

Work in pairs. Compete with your partner to write as many things as possible that are going on in the classroom, outside the window, or in a picture. Give yourselves two to three minutes. The person with the most sentences wins.

COMMUNICATIVE ACTIVITY 6

Role-Play

Work in pairs. Prepare a role-play for the following situation. Then perform it in front of the class.

Situation: Your friend is calling you to invite you for a coffee, but you don't feel like going. Reject the offer by saying that you are busy. Give a reason using the present progressive.

Reading

Read the passage and answer the questions that follow.

WHAT'S KEEPING KIDS FROM BEING MORE ACTIVE?

Are Kids Doing Enough Physical Activity These Days?

Everybody knows it is important to be physically active. Exercising or any other form of physical activity is an essential part of our lives. It <u>enhances</u> our health and helps us develop physical abilities. It's even more <u>crucial</u> in the proper physical and mental development of a child. An active child not only is healthy and weighs the right amount, but such a child also has high <u>self-esteem</u>. In contrast, an inactive child often <u>suffers</u> from <u>obesity</u> and has an increased risk of developing diseases as an adult.

These days, a lot of kids are not physically active enough. According to the Canadian Physical Activity <u>Guidelines</u>, children need to do some physical activities for at least 60 minutes per day. Instead, some surveys show that 46 percent of kids get three hours or less of active play per week, including weekends.

Usually in school, kids and youth have physical education classes, but these are often not on a daily basis or long enough. If kids do not have any other physical activity after school, then they are not meeting Canadian guidelines for their daily physical activity.

An additional problem is that kids are spending too much <u>sedentary</u> time at home. What are they doing? They are watching TV or playing computer or video games. That keeps them from playing outside and therefore being more active.

Some parents are trying to make sure their kids are getting enough exercise. They are asking their kids to play outside or signing them up for different sports activities. That way, the kids are moving and not sitting in front of the TV or a computer screen.

However, there are also some parents who are not letting their kids play outside because of the fear of something bad happening to them. If such parents still care about their kids' activity level, they choose organized sport activities for their kids or do some physical activities together as a family. For example, they take their kids for a walk, a swim, or a bike ride.

Parents' role in their kids' activity level is really big. They are the ones who <u>determine</u> if their kids are active enough or not. It's easy to let your kids stay home safely and spend time in front of a TV or a computer. However, a better option is for parents to organize physical activities for children, do them as a family, or even decide to lead by example and be physically active themselves.

COMPREHENSION

Answer the questions below. Write complete sentences.

1. Why is it important to be physically active?

   _____

2. What is the difference between an active and inactive child?

   _____

3. According to the Canadian Physical Activity Guidelines, how long do kids need to engage in physical activity?

   _____

4. Why aren't kids spending enough time being active? Give two reasons.

   _____

5. What are some parents doing to help their kids get more active?

   _____

6. Why aren't some parents letting their kids play outside?

   _____

7. What do some families do together to get physically active?

   _____

ANALYZING THE READING PASSAGE

Read the passage again and underline all the simple present tense verbs with a <u>single line</u> and all the present progressive tense verbs with a <u>double line</u>.

DISCUSSION

What is your opinion on this subject? Do you agree that kids are not active enough? Give some examples to support your opinion.

Listening 1

🔊 Track 09
Listen to the song. Fill in the blanks with the words you hear.

TOM'S DINER *by Suzanne Vega*

I _____
In the morning
At the diner
On the corner

I _____
At the counter
For the man
To pour the coffee

And he fills it
Only halfway
And before
I even argue

He _____
Out the window
At somebody
Coming in

"It is always
Nice to see you"
_____ the man
Behind the counter

To the woman
Who has come in
She _____
Her umbrella

And I look
The other way
As they _____
Their hellos and

I' _____
Not to see them
And instead
I pour the milk

I open
Up the paper
_____ a story
Of an actor

Who had died
While he was drinking
It was no one
I had heard of

And I' _____
To the horoscope
And looking
For the funnies

When I' _____
Someone watching me
And so
I raise my head

There's a woman
On the outside
_____ inside
Does she see me?

No she does not
Really see me
'Cause she sees
Her own reflection

And I' _____
Not to notice
That she's hitching
Up her skirt

And while she's
Straightening her stockings
Her hair
Has gotten wet

Oh, this rain
It will continue
Through the morning
As I' _____

To the bells
Of the cathedral . . .
I _____
Of your voice . . .

And of the
Midnight picnic
Once upon a time
Before the rain began

And I finish
Up my coffee
And it's time
To catch the train

COMPREHENSION

Listen to the song again and answer the following questions. Write complete sentences.
Use the present progressive tense.

1. Where is this person sitting right now? _____

2. What is she doing there? _____

3. Why is the man looking out the window? _____

4. What is the woman on the outside of the diner doing? _____

5. What is the weather like? _____

Listening 2

🔊 Track 10

BUSY OR NOT?

Listen to the audio. You will hear three phone conversations. In each of them, one person is calling and asking to speak to someone. Fill in the chart below. Write complete sentences.

Questions	Conversation 1	Conversation 2	Conversation 3
Is the person busy or not?			
What is the person doing?			
Is the person coming to the phone?			

Writing

Choose a photo of your own or use the one from Communicative Activity 2. On a separate sheet of paper, write a short composition (maximum 150 words) about the photo. Make sure you use the present progressive and the simple present verb tenses. Here are some questions to guide your writing:

- What do you see in the photo? Are there any people in the photo? Who are they?
- What are they doing?
- Why do you like / dislike the photo?
- Does the photo remind you of anything?

CHAPTER REVIEW

Summary

- The present progressive shows actions happening at the time of speaking, in progress, or in the near future.
- The keywords we use with the present progressive are *now*, *right now*, *at the moment*, *presently*, *currently*, and *this week*.
- We form the present progressive by using the verb *be* and then adding the verb with an *-ing* ending.
- There is a difference between the simple present and the present progressive.
- There are non-progressive verbs that we cannot use in the present progressive. Instead, we use the simple present with those verbs.

EXERCISE 1

Write questions in the present progressive. Use the words provided. Review the formation chart in this chapter on pages 58–59 if you need to.

Where / he / go? → Where is he going?

1. What / you / do / now? _____

2. Why / she / cry? _____

3. What kind of tea / he / drink? _____

4. How many kids / they / bring? _____

5. What / we / watch? _____

EXERCISE 2

There are five verb tense errors in the following passage. Find and correct them.

I really am liking fall. Right now, I am walk in a park and looking at the trees. They change colours now. I am seeing orange, red, and yellow leaves. Oh! And I am hearing how they crunch under my feet. I think fall is my favourite season.

EXERCISE 3

Change each of the following positive sentences into the negative. Review the formation chart in this chapter on pages 58–59 if you need to.

Elizabeth is teaching now. → Elizabeth is not teaching now.

1. He is swimming now.

   _____

2. We are skating at the Rideau Canal now.

   _____

3. You are buying a gift for your friend.

   _____

4. The printer is printing a document.

   _____

5. I am sitting at the park.

   _____

EXERCISE 4

Change each of the following sentences into a yes / no question. Review the formation chart in this chapter on pages 58–59 if you need to.

My dog is barking now. → **Is my dog barking now?**

1. Margaret is picking up her daughter from daycare now.

    _____?

2. Jose's dad is visiting his relatives in Europe this month.

    _____?

3. The doctor and the nurse are making rounds on the fourth floor now.

    _____?

4. My guests are coming in now.

    _____?

5. We are waiting in a lineup.

    _____?

EXERCISE 5

Change each of the following statements into a wh- question. The information you want to ask about is **in bold**. Review the formation charts in this chapter on pages 58–59 if you need to. For the list of question words, refer to Chapter 3, page 42.

The student is doing his homework now. → **What is the student doing now?**

1. Teresa is bothering **her brother**.

    _____?

2. Kim and Scott are getting married **this summer**.

    _____?

3. My siblings are preparing a party **for me**.

    _____?

4. You are paying **bills** at the bank now.

    _____?

5. The computer is making a noise **because it is broken**.

    _____?

Part 1 Review

Self-Study

OVERVIEW

The self-assessments in this unit give you a chance to review and reinforce the grammar points from Part 1 (Chapters 1–4).

Check your knowledge and if you find areas that need more attention, go back to the appropriate chapter and review the material.

EXERCISE 1

Unscramble the following words and make them into sentences or questions.

is / Her/ Jane / name → Her name is Jane.

1. languages / Some / difficult / are _____.

2. does / How much / cost / it _____?

3. two / has / He / dogs _____.

4. First / the / to / pre-heat / 260 degrees Celsius / oven

   _____.

5. Is / Mirek / on / sitting / the patio _____?

6. at / start / their / They / class / three o'clock / always

   _____.

7. do / need / an / you / When / umbrella _____?

8. car / is / That / mine _____.

9. yourself / it / Do / by _____.

10. Jonathan / her / gives / every / flowers / month

    _____.

EXERCISE 2

Change each of the following positive sentences into the negative.

I like it. → I do not like it.

1. Sit here. _____

2. These people are nice.

   _____

3. The average person laughs 15 times per day.

   _____

4. Henry has many friends.

   _____

5. My parents help me a lot.

   _____

EXERCISE 3

Change each of the following sentences into a yes / no question.

I am washing my hands now. → **Are you washing your hands now?**

1. My brother knows a lot about computers.

   _____?

2. My computer is working well today.

   _____?

3. Jake and Murako own a photo shop.

   _____?

4. Those women are coming back from church.

   _____?

5. We have many apple trees in our backyard.

   _____?

EXERCISE 4

Change each of the following statements into a Wh- question. The information you want to ask about is underlined and **in bold**.

She chats with her brother on Saturdays. → **When does she chat with her brother?**

1. Octopuses have **three** brains.

   _____?

2. Our actions are affecting **the future of our planet**.

   _____?

3. **Water** covers 70 percent of the earth's surface.

   _____?

4. For most people, it is impossible to sneeze with their eyes open **because sneezing is an involuntary nervous response**.

   _____?

5. Your heart **beats** more than 100,000 times a day.

   _____?

EXERCISE 5

Fill in the blanks with the correct form of the verbs in the present progressive or simple present.

Rita _____ (need) new shoes. She is at a shoe store now, and she

_____ (look) at some shoes.

Rita needs new shoes. She is at a shoe store now, and she is looking at some shoes.

Nick and Clara ₁ _____ (be) a young couple. They both ₂ _____

(work) full-time. Nick ₃ _____ (be) a financial adviser, and

Clara ₄ _____ (cook) for a restaurant. This weekend, Nick and Clara

₅ _____ (discuss) the future plans for their family. At the moment, they

₆ _____ (have, negative) any children, but they ₇ _____ (want)

to have some soon. Now, they ₈ _____ (look) at their photo albums from

their childhood and they ₉ _____ (having) fun. This is what they usually

₁₀ _____ (do) before making serious decisions.

EXERCISE 6

Correct the errors in the following sentences. The errors are <u>underlined</u>.

1. The dress is <u>fourty</u> dollars.

2. He is celebrating his <u>nineteen</u> birthday today.

3. I am a night person, but I never go to bed past <u>noon</u>.

4. Cats are <u>animals intelligent</u>.

5. <u>This</u> pencils belong to Sarah.

6. I like <u>mine</u> teacher.

7. How many <u>childs</u> do you have?

8. There <u>is</u> 20 students in Annie's class.

9. We have <u>many homeworks</u> to do for next week.

10. He has two <u>watchs</u>.

11. This house is <u>their</u>.

12. My husband works by <u>hisself</u>.

13. He lives in <u>an</u> house.

14. <u>The</u> money is important to some people.

15. My friends <u>goes</u> to Florida every winter.

16. She <u>haves</u> three children.

17. I <u>are</u> a plumber.

18. Suzanna is <u>writeing</u> a letter now.

19. <u>Do</u> Mark usually eat breakfast?

20. <u>Not talk</u> so loud!

Simple Past

OVERVIEW

The simple past expresses an action that is finished or completed in the past.

Use	Form	Keywords and Sample Phrases	Example Sentences
completed action	regular verbs: add -ed	yesterday **last** night **last** summer	I work**ed** yesterday. We watch**ed** TV last night. They travell**ed** last summer.
specific time in past	irregular verbs: memorize	two years **ago** in 1995 when I was a child	She **went** to Cuba two years ago. He **was born** in 1995. I **broke** my arm when I was a child.

Warm-up

Work in pairs. Read the first paragraph. <u>Underline</u> all the verbs. They are all in the simple present tense. List them in the chart below.

> Sasha and Norman are best friends. They walk to school together in the morning. They play together every day. They go to the park after school. They like the same sports. They always have fun.

Read the second version of the paragraph. <u>Underline</u> all the verbs. List them in the simple past tense column in the chart below. What do you notice about their forms? Can you see any patterns?

> Sasha and Norman were best friends. They walked to school together in the morning. They played together every day. They went to the park after school. They liked the same sports. They always had fun.

Simple Present Verbs	Simple Past Verbs	Observations

SIMPLE PAST—REGULAR VERBS

We form the simple past of most verbs by adding *-ed* to the base form of the verb.

Warm-up

Work in pairs. Read the following conversations aloud.

CONVERSATION 1

Partner A: What did you do last summer?
Partner B: I visited my family in Montreal.
Partner A: How long did you visit them for?
Partner B: I stayed there for a week.

CONVERSATION 2

Partner A: Did he watch TV yesterday?
Partner B: No, he didn't. He worked all day long.

CONVERSATION 3

Partner A: Did they study for their exam last weekend?
Partner B: Yes, they did. They studied for it last Sunday.

Read the warm-up conversations again. Notice that we know the exact timing of the actions in the past. What words or phrases show you that the action is in the past?

Formation

Positive	Negative	Question	Wh- Question
Subject + Verb (+ object / complement)	Subject + Auxiliary + Negative + Verb (+ object / complement)	Auxiliary + Subject + Verb (+ object / complement)	Question Word + Auxiliary + Subject + Verb (+ object / complement)
I **visited** my friend last summer.	I **did not visit** my friend last summer.	**Did** you **visit** your friend last summer?	**When** did you visit your friend?
You **stayed** there for a week.	You **did not stay** there for a week.	**Did** you **stay** there for a week?	**How long** did you stay there?
He **watched** them play.	He **did not watch** them play.	**Did** he **watch** them play?	**Who** did he watch play?
She **worked** last Friday.	She **did not work** last Friday.	**Did** she **work** last Friday?	**What** did she do last Friday?
It **started** at five o'clock.	It **did not start** at five o'clock.	**Did** it **start** at five o'clock?	**When** did it start?
We **decided** a week ago.	We **did not decide** a week ago.	**Did** we **decide** last Sunday?	**When** did we decide?
They **studied** last night.	They **did not study** last night.	**Did** they **study** last night?	**What** did they do last night?

- There is only **one** form of the verb for all persons (*I, you, he, she, it, we, they*) for all verbs except the verb *be*.
- Spelling rules for adding the *-ed* ending:
  - For a silent *-e* ending, add *-d* (arrive → arrived).
  - For a consonant + *y* ending, change the *y* to *i* and add *-ed* (study → studied).
  - To keep the short vowel sound between two consonants, double the final consonant (ban → banned).
- For the pronunciation of the *-ed* endings, see the chart before Exercise 2 on page 79.
- Remember to form wh- questions in the same way as yes / no questions. Use a question word and then add the rest of the question.

Note: See Chapter 3, page 42, the section Question Words for Wh- Questions. For a detailed explanation of how to form and use questions and negatives, refer to Chapter 11.

> Follow the same spelling rules for adding the *-ed* ending as for the *-s* ending in the simple present in Chapter 3 on page 44.

EXERCISE 1

Answer these questions with complete sentences.

> Did you talk with your teacher? → **Yes, I talked with my teacher.**
>
> Did she wash the dishes? → **No, she didn't wash the dishes.**

1. Did you visit any new places during your holiday?

   Yes, _____

2. Did John study the guitar at music camp last summer?

   No, _____

3. Did they travel outside Canada last year?

   Yes, _____

4. Did you work during the winter break last year?

   No, _____

5. Did Marie play volleyball last weekend?

   Yes, _____

PRONUNCIATION OF THE *-ED* ENDING

To make pronunciation easier, there are three ways to pronounce the *-ed* ending of past tense verbs.

Whether we use the /d/, /t/, or /id/ sound depends on the final sound of the verb's base form.

Remember it is the **sound** that matters, not the written letter.

Use the Sound	When the Final Sound of the Verb's Base Form Is	Examples
/d/ (voiced sounds)	a **vowel** sound or these consonant sounds: **b, g, j, l, m, n, ng, r, v, z, th, zh**	stay → stayed (stay/d/) follow → followed (follow/d/) try → tried (try/d/) bob → bobbed (bob/d/) fill → filled (fill/d/) buzz → buzzed (buzz/d/)

Use the Sound	When the Final Sound of the Verb's Base Form Is	Examples
/t/ (voiceless sounds)	these consonant sounds: **f, k, p, s, x, ch, sh, th**	look → looked (look/t/) hope → hoped (hope/t/) watch → watched (watch/t/)

Use the Sound	When the Final Sound of the Verb's Base Form Is	Examples
/id/	a **d** or **t** sound	end → ended (end/id/) want → wanted (want/id/)

EXERCISE 2

Place each verb from Exercise 1 in the correct column to show the pronunciation of the -*ed* ending.

/d/	/t/	/id/

⁂ COMMUNICATIVE ACTIVITY 1

Find the Order

Work in pairs or small groups. Put the following sentences in sequence to make a story. Write a number (1–10) next to each sentence to show the order.

_____ Michelle called her friends on Wednesday to invite them over.

_____ After dinner, they all enjoyed the cookies.

_____ On Saturday morning, Michelle cleaned her house, cooked a wonderful meal, and baked some cookies.

_____ Michelle welcomed her friends and offered them some drinks.

_____ At ten o'clock, they thanked Michelle for a great evening and returned home.

_____ At six o'clock, Michelle served dinner.

_____ They really liked the movie.

_____ Last week, Michelle decided to invite her friends Sylvie and Emma for dinner on Saturday.

_____ Sylvie and Emma arrived at Michelle's house at 5:30.

_____ Next, Michelle popped some popcorn, and they watched a movie.

SIMPLE PAST — IRREGULAR VERBS

Some verbs have irregular forms in the simple past. There is no rule for irregular verbs; you have to memorize them. However, there are some patterns.

Warm-up

Read the following passage. All the verbs are in the simple past tense. <u>Underline</u> them. (Circle) the verbs that do not end in -ed.

Last summer, my family planned to take a camping trip together, but it didn't happen that way. My parents bought a new tent and other camping equipment. They also rented two canoes. My mother organized the food, and I helped my father pack the van. We left early on the Friday morning. We got to the provincial park by 11:00 in the morning. Then we drove to the campsite. We all worked together; we set up the tent and the cooking area. Then my brother and I swam in the lake. When we came back to the campsite, we ate lunch. After lunch, we all went for a hike around the lakeshore. My father slipped on some loose rocks. He fell down and broke his ankle. We went back to the van, and my mother took Dad to the hospital. When they came back, we packed up our stuff and went home.

Formation

Positive	Negative	Question	Wh- Question
Subject + Verb (+ object / complement)	Subject + Auxiliary + Negative + Verb (+ object / complement)	Auxiliary + Subject + Verb (+ object / complement)	Question Word + Auxiliary + Subject + Verb (+ object / complement)
I **had** lunch.	I **did not have** lunch.	**Did** you **have** lunch?	**What** did you have?
You **wrote** a letter yesterday.	You **did not write** a letter yesterday.	**Did** you **write** a letter yesterday?	**When** did you write a letter?
He **spoke** to Ann.	He **did not speak** to Ann.	**Did** he **speak** to Ann?	**Who** did he speak to?
She **won**.	She **did not win**.	**Did** she **win**?	**What** did she do?
It **took** my shoe.	It **did not take** my shoe.	**Did** it **take** my shoe?	**What** did it take?
We **went** home.	We **did not go** home.	**Did** we **go** home?	**Where** did we go?
They **drove** to get to work.	They **did not drive** to get to work.	**Did** they **drive** to get to work?	**Why** did they drive?

Study the list of the common irregular past tense verbs in Appendix A. When you are ready, test yourself (or a partner) on the formation and spelling of the irregular verbs.

EXERCISE 3

Change these sentences into the simple past tense.

He goes to college. → He went to college.

1. You buy magazines. _____

2. I do my homework. _____

3. We go to the cinema. _____

4. He writes books. _____

5. They speak English very well. _____

EXERCISE 4

Change each of the following sentences into a yes / no question.

We **took** a trip to Newfoundland last summer. → **Did** you **take** a trip to Newfoundland last summer?

1. They went to Thailand two years ago.

   _____?

2. Meisha saw the Rocky Mountains on her trip out west.

   _____?

3. Paco and I flew to London to start our holiday.

   _____?

4. I bought a lot of souvenirs in Paris.

   _____?

5. Bupinder had a great time camping with his friends for a week.

   _____?

SIMPLE PAST—THE VERB *BE*

The verb *be* is also irregular in the simple past. There are two forms: *was* and *were*.

Warm-up

Prepare yes / no questions for your classmates. Use the five ideas below.
   Find someone who

- was absent yesterday.
- was born in another country.
- was tired this morning.
- was able to swim when he / she was a child.
- was happy last weekend.

On a separate sheet of paper, set up a chart like the one below and prepare some yes/no questions. Then ask some of your classmates the questions. If somebody answers "yes" to your question, record his or her name and write the answer in a complete sentence.

Questions	Names + Answers
Were you absent yesterday?	Kimiko was absent yesterday.

Formation

The verb *be* has two forms in the simple past tense. Notice that the third-person singular still has an *-s* ending.

I	was	we	were
he / she / it	was	you	were
		they	were

Positive	Negative	Question	Wh- Question
Subject + Verb + Complement	Subject + Verb + Negative + Complement	Verb + Subject + Complement	Question Word + Verb + Subject (+ complement)
I **was** a teacher in the past.	I **was not** a teacher in the past.	**Were** you a teacher in the past?	**Who** were you in the past?
You **were** sick.	You **were not** sick.	**Were** you sick?	**How** were you?
He **was** at home.	He **was not** at home.	**Was** he at home?	**Where** was he?
She **was** 10.	She **was not** 10.	**Was** she 10?	**How old** was she?
It **was** cold.	It **was not** cold.	**Was** it cold?	**How** was it?
We **were** there.	We **were not** there.	**Were** we there?	**Where** were we?
They **were** famous twins.	They **were not famous** twins.	**Were** they famous twins?	**Who** were they?

Remember that the verb *be* does not need an auxiliary verb to make negatives or questions.

EXERCISE 5

Fill in the blanks with the correct form of the verb *be* in the simple past tense.

You _____ (be) very nice.   You <u>were</u> very nice.

1. Anna _____ (**be**) away this weekend.

2. My brother and I _____ (**be**) happy to go with our parents on a family vacation.

3. (**be, question**) _____ they in the same class?

4. You _____ (**be, negative**) at home when I called you.

5. Daniel and Samuel _____ (**be**) very good students.

⚜ COMMUNICATIVE ACTIVITY 2

Exchange Information

Work in pairs. Read the following paragraph about Debbie's childhood. Then, tell your partner about yourself when you were a child, using the verb *be*. After, record some facts about your partner's childhood and yours in a chart on a separate sheet of paper. Ask each other questions to get more information.

Debbie **was** born in Canada, but her parents **were** Polish. They always spoke Polish at home. When Debbie **was** six years old, she started Grade 1. She **was** a tall girl, so everybody thought she **was** seven or eight years old. She **was** also very smart. She **was** able to write well, read fluently in English, and say some words in French. Her teachers **were** happy to have Debbie in their classes. Also, all her friends really liked her. When she got an excellent report card at the end of the year, her parents **were** very proud of her.

You	Your Partner

BRINGING IT ALL TOGETHER

⚜ COMMUNICATIVE ACTIVITY 3

Video Summary

In small groups, watch a 10- to 15-minute video or movie segment of your choice (from the Internet, TV, or library). Write a short summary of what happened, step by step, in the simple past. Words that indicate time and sequence are listed below to help you write your summary. When you finish, one group member reads the summary aloud while a different group member lists the verb forms used. Make sure to write down both the simple past and the base form of each verb.

first	then	finally
in the beginning	next	at the end
to start	afterward	the conclusion

COMMUNICATIVE ACTIVITY 4

Telling Stories about the Weekend

Work as a class. One student leaves the classroom while the teacher tells what he or she did last weekend. The remaining students take notes, trying to write the main points, using verbs in the simple past. When the teacher finishes the story, the student who has left returns to the classroom. Each person who heard the story says one sentence about it or describes an action from it. The returning student tries to tell the whole story back to the class. If he or she makes any mistakes, the others should make corrections. After, all the students write out the whole story.

(This activity can also be done with students telling about their weekends.)

COMMUNICATIVE ACTIVITY 5

Spelling Bee

Work in small teams. The teacher will give each team a list of verbs. Taking turns, a team chooses a verb from their list, and one member of another team has to spell the past tense of the verb. This can be done orally or by writing on the board. If the spelling is correct, that student's team scores a point. If not, then another team gets a chance to spell it correctly and steal the point.

Reading

Read the passage and answer the questions that follow.

OUR CANADA DAY

July 1st, Canada Day, two years ago was the first time we celebrated this holiday in Ottawa. My husband, Larry, my two children, Karl and Alan, and I stayed in Ottawa to be part of Canada's birthday celebration.

We got up early in the morning and walked to the ByWard Market. The market was still quiet. The <u>vendors</u> were busy. They needed to set up their <u>stalls</u>. We wanted to have breakfast in a café. We found a little café with a patio where we ate a delicious breakfast of fresh fruit, croissants, and hot chocolate.

After breakfast we walked around and looked at all of the market stalls. The vendors had a wide variety of things for sale: fresh fruit and vegetables, jewellery, clothing, and <u>souvenirs</u>.

The morning passed very quickly. For lunch, we decided to buy food and have a picnic in one of the many outdoor sitting areas. We ate our food and watched all of the other families enjoying this national holiday.

In the afternoon, we decided to take a boat <u>cruise</u> on the Rideau Canal because Karl and Alan were tired from walking. During the tour, we saw many large houses and beautiful gardens.

For dinner, Karl and Alan wanted to buy sausages from a street vendor. We ate dinner sitting on a park bench. What fun!

After dinner, we walked to Parliament Hill. It was very <u>crowded</u>. The music and <u>entertainment</u> were very enjoyable. The <u>fireworks</u> provided the <u>grand finale</u> for the day.

Karl, Alan, Larry, and I walked home, tired but happy after spending our first Canada Day in Ottawa.

COMPREHENSION

Answer the questions. Use complete sentences.

1. What is the date of Canada's birthday?

    _____

2. How many children does the writer have?

    _____

3. Where did the family celebrate Canada Day?

    _____

4. Where did the family have breakfast?

    _____

5. What did the family have for breakfast?

    _____

6. What did the vendors have for sale in their stalls?

    _____

7. What did the family do in the afternoon? Why?

    _____

8. Where did the family eat dinner?

    _____

9. What did the family have for dinner?

    _____

10. Where did the family go after dinner?

_____

11. What did the family do in the evening?

_____

12. Did the family have an enjoyable day?

_____

ANALYZING THE READING PASSAGE

Read the passage again. Underline all the regular past tense verbs with a <u>single line</u> and all the irregular ones with a <u>double line</u>.

CLASS DISCUSSION

Did you celebrate Canada Day with your family or friends last year? What did you do?

Listening

◀)) Track 11

CANADA DAY IN OTTAWA

Listen to the audio and answer the questions that follow.

COMPREHENSION

Write complete sentences. Use the simple past tense.

1. Did Karl and Alan have a good day? _____

2. Who enjoyed the croissants? _____

3. Did the two boys swim? _____

4. Did Alan buy a rope bracelet? _____

5. What did they have for lunch? _____

6. Where did they buy lunch? _____

7. Where did they eat lunch? _____

8. What did they buy from a street vendor? _____

9. What did they see on Parliament Hill? _____

10. Were there a lot of people on Parliament Hill? _____

Writing

Choose one of the topics below. Write a short composition (maximum 150 words) about the topic.

- What did you do last summer?
- What is your favourite holiday or childhood memory?

CHAPTER REVIEW

Summary

- The simple past shows a completed action in the past.
- Certain keywords or phrases, such as *last year*, *ago*, or *when I was young*, tell you the action was completed in the past.
- All the verbs, except *be*, have only one form in the simple past. For regular verbs, add *-ed* to the base form. You need to memorize irregular verbs.
- All the verbs, except *be*, need to use *did* and the base form of the verb to create questions and negatives.
- The verb *be* has two forms in the simple past: *was* (*I*, *he*, *she*, *it*) and *were* (*you*, *we*, *they*).
- To create questions with the verb *be*, change the order of the subject and verb.

    s.   v.   v.   s.
He was there.   Was he there?

- To create negatives, add *not* after *be*. Do not use *did* with *be*.

    He wasn't there.

EXERCISE 1

Fill in the blanks with the correct form of the simple past of the verbs in parentheses.

Where _____ (go, they) on Saturday?

Where <u>did they go</u> on Saturday?

1. Jonathan _____ (**move**) to Sherbrooke two years ago.

2. When Frank _____ (**be**) young, he _____ (**want**) to be an astronaut.

3. Amanda _____ (**study**) Spanish for two years before she _____ (**go**) to Spain.

4. When _____ (meet, you) Alan?

5. I _____ (know, not) how to swim until I _____ (be) 20.

EXERCISE 2

Use the words provided to write wh- questions. You need to add an auxiliary verb or change the form of the verb. Review the formation charts in this chapter on pages 77, 81, and 83 if you need to. For a detailed explanation of how to form and use wh- questions, refer to Chapter 11. A chart of question words is in Chapter 3 on page 42.

Why / he / leave / early? → Why did he leave early?

1. How / you / get / here? _____?

2. Where / she / be / born? _____?

3. When / they / write / exams? _____?

4. What movie / she / see / last night? _____?

5. What countries / you / visit / last summer? _____?

EXERCISE 3

Change each of the following positive sentences into the negative. Review the formation charts in this chapter on pages 77, 81, and 83 if you need to.

I smiled at him. → I did not smile at him.

We ate lunch an hour ago. → We did not eat lunch an hour ago.

They were there last year. → They were not there last year.

1. He called her at five o'clock. _____

2. She was in Europe in 2010. _____

3. Claire visited her parents last month. _____

4. I took my dog for a walk this morning. _____

5. They bought a new house two years ago. _____

EXERCISE 4

Change each of the following statements into a wh- question. The information you want to ask about is **in bold**. Review the formation charts in this chapter on pages 77, 81, and 83 and the question word list on page 42 in Chapter 3 if you need to.

He walked to school **this morning.** → When did he walk to school?

They went **to Sweden** last summer. → Where did they go last summer?

I was absent **because I had an appointment.** → Why were you absent?

Julietta enjoyed **the concert.** → What did Julietta enjoy?

Remember: The word order for wh- questions is usually the same as for yes / no questions.

1. He travelled **to Alaska** in 2001. _____?

2. Marie drew that picture **when she was six years old**.

   _____?

3. They arrived in Kingston **by train** at 8 o'clock.

   _____?

4. They were **16 years old** when they met. _____?

5. Sophie packed **her bag** before she left for school.

   _____?

EXERCISE 5

Fill in the blanks in this letter with the simple past tense of the verbs in parentheses.

Dear Julie,

I ₁ _____ (read) about your vacation in Montreal during the summer. We ₂ _____ (go) to Toronto for a weekend.

   We ₃ _____ (leave) at 8:00 in the morning. The drive on Highway 401 ₄ _____ (be) good. An accident ₅ _____ (happen) around Belleville, so we ₆ _____ (stop) at the new rest stop on the 401 and ₇ _____ (have) a coffee.

   We ₈ _____ (arrive) in Toronto at 3:00 in the afternoon. We ₉ _____ (drive) to our hotel and ₁₀ _____ (unpack) our luggage.

   We ₁₁ _____ (eat) dinner in a restaurant next to the hotel. We ₁₂ _____ (see) a play at one of big theatres. It ₁₃ _____ (be) fun.

   The next day, we ₁₄ _____ (take) the ferry to the Toronto Islands for the afternoon.

   We ₁₅ _____ (order) dinner in a small Greek restaurant. On Sunday, we ₁₆ _____ (visit) Kensington Market and had breakfast. After breakfast we ₁₇ _____ (pay) the bill and we ₁₈ _____ (go) to the Ontario Science Centre. Later, we ₁₉ _____ (return) to the hotel. We ₂₀ _____ (check) out, ₂₁ _____ (pack) the car, and ₂₂ _____ (begin) our journey back to Ottawa.

   We ₂₃ _____ (have) a great weekend.

Your friend,

Martha

Past Progressive

OVERVIEW

- Remember, the simple past expresses an action that ended in the past.
- The past progressive expresses
  - actions that were happening during a limited time in the past.
  - temporary actions in the past.
  - actions in progress in the past when another action happened or interrupted.
  - actions each in progress at the same time in the past.

Use	Form	Keywords	Example Sentences
limited time		last month last week last night on Friday on the weekend	I was studying last night. I was visiting my family on the weekend.
temporary actions	*was* / *were* + base form of a verb + *-ing* (present participle)	at that moment right then	She was eating an apple right then.
actions in progress when another action happens		while, as when (used with the simple past)	While we were walking in the park, we met Henry. He was taking a shower when she telephoned.
actions in progress at the same time		while, as	While you were sleeping, I was studying.

Warm-up

Work in pairs. Read the first paragraph below. Together, <u>underline</u> all the verbs. List them in order in the first row of the chart below.

Right now, Sergei and Kumar are sitting on the patio at the café. It is a beautiful day. They are waiting for their friends, Shanda and Meisha. They want to make plans for Saturday night. They are planning a surprise party for Martine's birthday.

Read the second version of the paragraph. Together, <u>underline</u> all the verbs. List them in order in the second row of the chart.

Yesterday, Sergei and Kumar were sitting on the patio at the café. It was a beautiful day. They were waiting for their friends, Shanda and Meisha. They wanted to make plans for Saturday night. They were planning a surprise party for Martine's birthday.

Paragraph 1					
Paragraph 2					

Compare the verbs in the first row with the verbs in the second row. What do you notice about their forms? Can you see any patterns?

PAST PROGRESSIVE

We form the past progressive of regular verbs by combining the past tense of *be* with the present participle (or *-ing* form) of the verb.

Warm-up

Work in pairs. Read the following conversation aloud.

Partner A: Hi, Sandra. I thought I saw you late last night at the college. What were you doing?
Partner B: I was studying in the library, but I fell asleep.
Partner A: It was quite late. How did you get home?
Partner B: I missed the last bus, so I was waiting for my friend to come to get me in his car. He was working when I called him. What were you doing there so late?
Partner A: I was walking by the college on my way home from work.

Read the conversation again. <u>Underline</u> all the verbs. Write them in the correct column in a chart on a separate piece of paper.

Simple Past	Past Progressive
thought	were doing

Read the conversation a third time. Can you guess why the simple past is used for some actions and the past progressive is used for others?

Formation

Positive	Negative	Question	Wh- Question
Subject + *be* + Verb -*ing* (+ object / complement)	Subject + *be* + Negative + Verb -*ing* (+ object / complement)	*Be* + Subject + Verb -*ing* (+ object / complement)	Question Word + *be* + Subject + Verb -*ing* (+ object / complement)
I **was** study**ing** yesterday.	I **was not** study**ing** yesterday.	**Were** you study**ing** yesterday?	**When** were you studying?
You **were eating** supper.	You **were not** eat**ing** supper.	**Were** you eat**ing** supper?	**What** were you eating?
He **was** sleep**ing** on the sofa.	He **was not** sleep**ing** on the sofa.	**Was** he sleep**ing** on the sofa?	**Where** was he sleeping?
She **was** play**ing** a video game.	She **was not** play**ing** a video game.	**Was** she play**ing** a video game?	**What** was she playing?
It **was** snow**ing**.	It **was not** snow**ing**.	**Was** it snow**ing**?	**What** was it doing?
We **were** sit**ting** in the front row.	We **were not** sit**ting** in the front row.	**Were** you sit**ting** in the front row?	**Where** were you sitting?
They **were** talk**ing** on the phone.	They **were not** talk**ing** on the phone.	**Were** they talk**ing** on the phone?	**How** were they talking?

Note:

- Remember that wh- questions have the same structure as yes / no questions. The question word replaces specific information in the yes / no question. Write the question word and add the rest of the question.
- Follow the formation rules for *be* for questions and negatives in the past progressive.

- For a detailed explanation of how to form and use questions and negatives, refer to Chapter 11.
- To review the spelling rules for verbs with the *-ing* ending, see Chapter 4, page 59.

We often join the verb *be* and *not,* and the auxiliary verb and *not,* to form contractions or shorter forms. We join the two words together and use an apostrophe (') to replace the letter *o.*

Be + *not*	Auxiliary + *not*
is not → isn't	does not → doesn't
are not → aren't	do not → don't
was not → wasn't	did not → didn't
were not → weren't	

- *I am not* is the exception. We make a contraction only with the pronoun *I* because a contraction with *not* is too difficult to pronounce.

   I am not → I'm not

Refer to Appendix B for a complete chart of the contractions used with the verb tenses presented in this book.

EXERCISE 1

Fill in the blanks with the past progressive form of the verbs in parentheses.

While I _____ (make) supper, my friend called.

While I <u>was making</u> supper, my friend called.

1. Last Sunday, we _____ (come) home on the bus.

2. Paul _____ (talk, not) to his friend.

3. They _____ (begin) to do their homework.

4. Marie-Josée _____ (hum) a song.

5. _____ it _____ (rain)?

EXERCISE 2

Answer these questions. Use complete sentences.

Were you listening to the songs on your MP3 player? → **Yes, I was** listening to the songs on my MP3 player.

Was she dancing? → **No,** she was not dancing.

1. Was Maria chatting with her friend on the phone?

   Yes, ————————————————————————————————————

2. Were you doing your homework?

   No, ————————————————————————————————————

3. Were John and Isabel playing cards in the cafeteria?

   Yes, ————————————————————————————————————

4. Were you and your friend walking downtown on Saturday afternoon?

   Yes, ————————————————————————————————————

5. Was Malek playing soccer with his friends?

   No, ————————————————————————————————————

 ## COMMUNICATIVE ACTIVITY 1

Describing a Picture

Work in pairs. Look at the picture of people in a restaurant. First, write your own sentences to describe what was happening in the restaurant at noon yesterday. Use the past progressive. After three to five minutes, share your sentences with your partner. Then share your sentences with other pairs. Below are some verbs to help you get started.

talk	order	sit
wait for	serve	stand
look at	carry	walk

PAST PROGRESSIVE VERSUS SIMPLE PAST

Warm-up

Walk around the class and interview three students. Ask the following questions, and record your answers in the chart. Share your findings with the rest of the class.

Look at the example to help you.

Henrik stayed home last night. At 6:00 PM, he was taking a nap. While he was taking a nap, the phone rang.

Questions	Student 1	Student 2	Student 3
1. What did you do last night?			
2. What were you doing at 6:00 last night? Did anything happen while you were doing that?			
3. What were you doing at 8:30 last night? Did anything happen while you were doing that?			
4. What were you doing at 11:00 last night? Did anything happen while you were doing that?			

Formation

They were playing soccer when it started to rain.

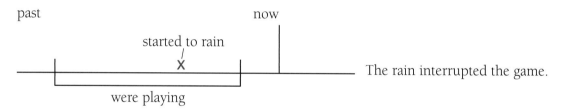

The rain interrupted the game.

While I was taking a shower, the phone rang.

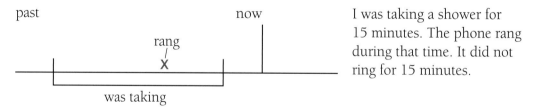

I was taking a shower for 15 minutes. The phone rang during that time. It did not ring for 15 minutes.

Both actions are in the past. The past progressive action happened over a limited time in the past. The simple past action interrupted or happened during the other action. Remember that *while* and *as* are usually the keywords or the signals to use the past progressive. *When* is usually the keyword for the simple past.

Remember that certain verbs cannot be used in the present progressive tense. The same rule applies to the past progressive tense. The non-progressive verbs include verbs that express the senses, emotions, mental actions, possession, and existence. Review the non-progressive verb chart on pages 61–62 in Chapter 4.

EXERCISE 3

Fill in the blanks with the correct form of the verbs in parentheses. Use the past progressive or the simple past.

While I _____ (wash) the dishes, someone _____ (ring) the doorbell.

While I <u>was washing</u> the dishes, someone <u>rang</u> the doorbell.

1. Yan _____ (meet) his wife while they _____ (go) to university.

2. Susan _____ (fix) her bicycle when her friend _____ (drop) by.

3. When she _____ (hear) the noise, she _____ (look) out the window to see what _____ (happen).

4. While we _____ (fly) to Vancouver, there _____ (be) a terrible thunderstorm.

5. I _____ (walk) down the street when I _____ (find) a wallet.

EXERCISE 4

Change each of the following statements into a wh- question. The information you want to ask about is **in bold**. Refer to the formation chart on page 93 and the question word list on page 42 in Chapter 3 if you need to. Note: For a detailed explanation of how to form and use questions, refer to Chapter 11. Look at the examples to help you.

The student was doing **his homework** in the library. → **What** was the student doing in the library?

We cooked the chicken **while she was cleaning the house.** → **When** did you cook chicken?

They were **sleeping** at midnight. → **What** were they doing at midnight?

1. Juan **was playing basketball** when I saw him.

   _____?

2. Angelica came to visit us **while we were packing for our trip**.

   _____?

3. I was driving **to the store** when I saw the accident.

   _____?

4. The students were checking **their emails** before the teacher arrived.

   _____?

5. **Seven** students were still writing the exam when the fire alarm rang.

   _____?

✥ COMMUNICATIVE ACTIVITY 2

Scrambled Parts

Work in small groups. Your teacher will give each group four piles of cards with words on them. Arrange the cards from each pile to form complete sentences. The group that finishes first and has the most correct answers wins.

BRINGING IT ALL TOGETHER

✥ COMMUNICATIVE ACTIVITY 3

Freeze Frame

Work in teams. Write down action verbs to act out, such as "scratching your head" or "yawning." Write one or two action verbs for each person in your group, depending on the time allowed by your teacher. You can act them out alone or as a group. Your teacher will ask a team to act out an action. After 10 seconds, your teacher will say "stop" or "freeze." Hold your positions. The teacher will ask another team to answer the question, "What was he or she doing?" or "What were they doing?" If the team doesn't guess correctly, the teacher will ask the student, "What were you doing?" The teams take turns acting out the actions. The team with the most correct answers wins.

✥ COMMUNICATIVE ACTIVITY 4

Video Summary

Work in pairs. Your teacher will show a short video clip. Pay attention to what is happening in the video. When your teacher stops the video, write as many sentences as you can describing the action in the video. Use the past progressive and the simple past. Compare your sentences with your partner's. Did you miss any actions? Read your sentences aloud to another pair of students.

> A fable is a very short story with a moral or lesson. Fables often have animals or things as the characters, such as in "The Tortoise and the Hare."

Reading

Read the fable and answer the questions that follow.

ANDROCLES

A very long time ago, a <u>slave</u> named Androcles <u>escaped</u> from his master and ran away to the forest. While he was <u>wandering</u> in the forest, he saw a lion. The lion was lying down; he was moaning in pain. At first, Androcles turned to run away, but when the lion did not chase him, Androcles turned back and went up to the lion. As he was coming near, the lion put out his <u>paw</u>; it was <u>swollen</u> and it was bleeding. Androcles found a huge <u>thorn</u> in it, and that thorn was causing all the pain. He pulled out the thorn and bandaged the paw of the lion. The lion was <u>grateful</u> and was soon able to rise and lick the hand of Androcles. Then the lion took Androcles to his cave. Every day, the lion brought him meat to eat. However, a short time later, the Emperor's men found both Androcles and the lion and took them back to the Emperor. To punish Androcles for escaping, the Emperor ordered the soldiers to put him into an arena with the lion. The lion was very hungry. The Emperor and all his Court came to see the slave and the lion fight. The soldiers led Androcles into the middle of the arena. Then they opened the lion's cage. When the lion rushed out, he was <u>roaring</u> and racing toward his victim. But as he was approaching Androcles, he recognized his friend. The lion knelt down to Androcles, and licked his hands like a friendly dog. The Emperor was very surprised at this. He called Androcles to come to him. Androcles told the Emperor the whole story. As a result, the Emperor pardoned and freed Androcles. He also set the lion free to live in his native forest. The moral is that "gratitude is the sign of noble souls," which means we should be thankful when someone helps us and repay that kindness.

Adapted from three versions of *Aesop's Fables*: www.aesopfables.com/cgi/aesop1.cgi?1&Androcles and www.taleswith morals.com/aesop-fable-androcles.htm and www.pagebypagebooks.com/Aesop/Aesops_Fables/Androcles_p1.html.

COMPREHENSION

Answer the questions. Use complete sentences.

1. Who did Androcles meet in the forest?

   _____

2. Why was the lion moaning in pain?

   _____

3. What did the Emperor do to punish Androcles for escaping?

   _____

4. When did the lion recognize his friend?

   _____

5. What did the Emperor decide to do in the end?

   _____

ANALYZING THE READING PASSAGE

Read the fable again. Underline all the simple past tense verbs with a <u>single line</u>. Then underline all the past progressive tense verbs with a <u>double line</u>.

DISCUSSION

Stories, such as fables and legends, are passed on from one generation to another in all cultures. Can you think of any stories you heard as a child? Do you think this kind of story still provides us with good lessons today?

Listening

🔊 Track 12

MYTHS AND LEGENDS

Listen to the audio and answer the questions that follow.

COMPREHENSION

Circle the letter of the correct answer.

1. What was the man doing when he heard about the new radio series?
   a) He was working.
   b) He was listening to the radio at home.
   c) He was driving home.

2. What is the subject of the new radio series?
   a) First Nations and Inuit storytelling and legends
   b) legends and myths
   c) fairy tales and fables

3. What were the people on the radio saying?
   a) They were telling a First Nations legend.
   b) They were listening to a First Nations legend.
   c) They were explaining the differences between legends, myths, and fables.

4. What do fables always have?
   a) historical facts
   b) a lesson
   c) animals and people

5. What are myths?
   a) They are stories based on historical facts.
   b) They are stories created long ago to explain things.
   c) They are stories with animals and things that speak and act like people.

6. According to the audio, what story is an example of a myth?
   a) *Hercules*
   b) *Cinderella*
   c) *Robin Hood*

7. Why did the speaker say that *Robin Hood* is a legend?
   a) All of the people and places are real.
   b) None of the people and places are real.
   c) Some of the people and places are real.

8. According to the audio, what story is an example of a fairy tale?
   a) *Hercules*
   b) *Cinderella*
   c) *Robin Hood*

9. What does the speaker think the First Nations stories are?
   a) legends
   b) myths
   c) both legends and myths

10. When does the new radio series begin?
    a) today
    b) next week
    c) next month

Writing

The following is the beginning of a story. On a separate piece of paper, write approximately 10 sentences to finish the story. It can be a serious or a silly story. Use the past progressive and the simple past.

As I was walking down the street the other day, I saw a young man. He was sitting on the steps in front of an apartment building. He was singing and playing the guitar. In front of the next building, there were two boys. They were . . .

CHAPTER REVIEW

Summary

- The past progressive expresses
  - actions that were happening during a limited time in the past.
  - temporary actions in the past.
  - actions in progress in the past when another action happened or interrupted.
  - actions each in progress at the same time in the past.

- The simple past expresses an action that is finished or completed in the past.
- *While* and *as* are usually the keywords or the signals to use the past progressive.
- *When* is usually the keyword for the simple past.
- Remember that we cannot use non-progressive verbs in the past progressive tense. The non-progressive verbs include verbs that express the senses, emotions, mental actions, possession, and existence. Review the non-progressive verb chart on pages 61–62 in Chapter 4.

EXERCISE 1

Change the verbs in the following paragraph from the present to the past. Change the simple present tense verbs to the simple past. Change the present progressive tense verbs to the past progressive.

When I arrive home from work, my roommate is preparing supper. While I am changing my clothes, he says we need to study for an exam. While we are eating our meal, we start to ask each other questions about the exam. We are studying while we are having our supper. We continue to ask questions while we are doing the dishes. By the time we finish the dishes, we know what things we need to review. I like to study that way.

EXERCISE 2

There are five errors in the use of the past progressive or the simple past in the following paragraph. Find and correct them.

I was hearing a story on the radio about why the Native people began to make dream catchers. One day, an old woman was watch a spider. The spider was spinning its web. The woman's grandson wanted to kill the spider, but she was stopping him. The spider was so grateful that he showed the woman how to make a web. While it showed her how to do it, the spider explained that only good dreams passed through the web. The web was trapping all the bad dreams.

EXERCISE 3

Use the words provided to write sentences or questions in the past progressive. You need to change the verb into the past progressive. Review the formation chart in this chapter on page 93 if you need to.

Where / he / go? → Where was he going?

1. The singer / sing / my favourite song.

   _____

2. Frank and his friends / play / soccer?

   _____

3. Samantha / take / the bus to work.

   _____

4. the children / feed / some animals at the zoo?

   _____

5. my friend / cut / my hair.

   _____

EXERCISE 4

Change each of the following sentences into a yes / no question. Review the formation chart in this chapter on page 93 if you need to.

My dog was barking at that moment. → Was my dog barking at that moment?

1. It was raining at 10:00 last night.

   _____?

2. We were trying to find the answer to the question.

   _____?

3. I was sewing a button on my shirt.

   _____?

4. The players were waiting for the game to begin.

   _____?

5. Guillermo was taking a nap.

   _____?

EXERCISE 5

Circle the letter of the correct word or phrase to complete the sentences.

1. George was talking on the phone _____ I got home.
   a) when
   b) while

2. It _____ when I left work.
   a) rained
   b) was raining

3. The man _____ to catch the bus when I saw him.
   a) ran
   b) was running

4. While you were sleeping, I _____ to the store.
   a) went
   b) was going

5. When the teacher explained the lesson, I _____ it.
   a) understood
   b) was understanding

EXERCISE 6

Change each of the following positive sentences into the negative. Review the formation chart in this chapter on page 93 if you need to. Look at the example to help you.

Elizabeth was teaching yesterday. → Elizabeth was not (wasn't) teaching yesterday.

1. I was speaking to my boss about the problem at work.

   _____

2. Yesterday, we were studying for the test.

   _____

3. She was walking the dog at that time.

   _____

4. They were watching the movie on TV.

   _____

5. We were celebrating our anniversary at the restaurant.

   _____

Adjectives and Adverbs

OVERVIEW

- Adjectives are parts of speech that describe nouns or pronouns.

- When we compare two things, we use comparative adjectives.

- When we describe three or more things and state that one of them is of the highest or lowest degree, we use superlative adjectives.

- Adverbs describe verbs and modify adjectives or other adverbs.

- When we compare two actions, we use comparative adverbs.

- When we talk about three or more actions, we use superlative adverbs.

- When we want to express that two things or actions are the same, we use equative adjectives and adverbs.

Warm-up

Read the following proverbs and their explanations. Underline any adjectives with a <u>single line</u> and any adverbs with a <u>double line</u>.

Good conscience is a soft pillow. = You sleep nicely if you are not guilty of anything.

A bad tree does not yield good apples. = If you are a bad parent, most likely your kids are bad too.

A good management is better than a good income. = You can lose your money fast if you do not manage it well.

Be swift to hear, slow to speak. = Listen carefully before you speak.

A good example is the best sermon. = It's better to show by doing than by giving advice.

Great oaks grow from small acorns. = Some things start really small before they become big and well known.

Love is blind. = A person in love often can't see the negative sides of the person he or she loves.

Nobody is perfect. = Everyone makes mistakes.

The first step is the hardest. = It's hard to start something.

ADJECTIVES

Warm-up

Think of three nouns. In the chart below, write those nouns in the first column. Then, in the second column, write a word that describes each of those nouns.

Noun	A Word That Describes the Noun
house	new
classmates	funny

Formation

Formation	Example Sentences
Adjectives modify or qualify nouns or pronouns.	A **bad** tree does not yield **good** apples. It's **hard** to start something.
We place adjectives before a noun or after the verbs *be* or *become*.	**Good** conscience is a **soft** pillow. Love is **blind**. They become **big** and **well known**.
Adjectives are always singular even if the noun or pronoun is plural.	**Great** oaks grow from **small** acorns.

EXERCISE 1

Describe each of the following people or things. Use at least three adjectives. Write complete sentences.

oranges: Oranges are **orange, round,** and **sweet.**

1. athletes

   _____

2. babies

   _____

3. cats

   _____

4. school

   _____

5. this book

   _____

⁂ COMMUNICATIVE ACTIVITY 1

A Good Friend Is . . .

Work in pairs. Look at the examples of some qualities that make a good friend on the next page. By yourself, order them from 1 (very important) to 10 (not very important). Share your list with your partner, and explain the reasons for choosing this order. Then, add other qualities that are not on the list but are important to you both.

——— honest	——— intelligent
——— funny	——— well behaved
——— reliable	——— forgiving
——— unselfish	——— attentive
——— energetic	——— generous

Other qualities _____

ADVERBS

Warm-up

On a separate piece of paper, make a two-column chart like the one started below. Think of three verbs. Write those verbs in the first column. Then, in the second column, write a word that describes each of those verbs.

Verb	A Word That Describes the Verb
laugh	loudly
run	fast

Formation

Formation	Example Sentences
Adverbs modify or qualify verbs, adjectives, or other adverbs.	Listen **carefully** before you speak. Some things start **really** small before they become big and well known. She drives **extremely carefully**.
We use adjectives to form adverbs. A general rule is to add -ly to the end of an adjective.	Louis is a **slow** eater. Louis eats **slowly**. That was a **quick** answer. He answered it **quickly**. It was an **informal** conversation. We spoke **informally**.
For adjectives ending with e, add -ly.	She has **nice** clothes. She dresses **nicely**.

For adjectives ending with a consonant + *y*, change *y* to *i*, and add *-ly*.	They have a **happy** life. They live **happily**.
For adjectives ending with *le*, delete *e* and add *-y*.	My new sofa is **comfortable**. I am sitting **comfortably** on my new sofa.
For adjectives ending with *ic* add *-ally*.	Cecile is a **sympathetic** listener. She always listens to others **sympathetically**.
There are also irregular adverbs.	Eerie is a **good** singer. Eerie sings **well**. Those players are **fast**. They play **fast**. Brian is a **hard** worker. He works **hard**.

EXERCISE 2

Change each of the following adjectives into an adverb.

1. quiet _____
2. easy _____
3. terrible _____
4. perfect _____
5. safe _____

6. tragic _____
7. hard _____
8. good _____
9. soft _____
10. basic _____

 ## COMMUNICATIVE ACTIVITY 2

What's the Adverb?

Work in pairs. Look back at Communicative Activity 1. There are six adjectives that you can change to adverbs. Make a sentence with each of those adverbs.

honest → honestly   Sentence: My friend always speaks honestly.

COMPARATIVE ADJECTIVES

We use comparative adjectives to compare **two** things, places, people, or groups of people. Comparative adjectives show us how those **two** things are different.

Warm-up

Work in pairs. Look at the groups of photos. Try to compare the people and the objects you see in the photos. Use adjectives.

Can you guess how we form comparative adjectives?

Formation

Adjective Types	Examples	Formation	Example Sentences
one-syllable adjectives	tall	Add -er.	Xiang is **taller than** Micha.
one-syllable adjectives ending with an e	nice	Add -r.	Today is **nicer than** yesterday.
one-syllable adjectives ending with a consonant-vowel-consonant	big	Double the last consonant, and add -er.	Their house is **bigger than** ours.
two-syllable adjectives ending with a y	busy	Change y to i and add -er.	York Street is **busier than** Park Avenue.
adjectives with two or more syllables	creative	Insert more or less before the adjective.	Carl is **more creative than** Sam. Sam is **less creative than** Carl.
irregular adjectives	good bad far (distance)	No rules; memorize those adjectives.	Water is **better than** juice. This car is **worse than** that one. My school is **farther than** your school from here.

*Farther relates to distance and further relates to degree.   **Do you need further explanation?**

The comparative adjective is often followed by the word than.

EXERCISE 3

Fill in the blanks with the comparative form of the adjectives in parentheses. Note that the example below has two possible answers.

You are _____ (athletic) than he is. → You are <u>more athletic</u> than he is.

→ You are <u>less athletic</u> than he is.

1. Juan's desk seems to be _____ (neat) than Meagan's.

2. Trent is _____ (young) than his brother Travis.

3. Children are often _____ (happy) than adults because they don't have many things to worry about.

4. My cousin likes sports, but I like art. When we paint, my cousin is _____ (artistic) than I am.

5. Are dogs _____ (smart) than cats?

SUPERLATIVE ADJECTIVES

Superlative adjectives express the extreme quality of one thing out of many things or a group of things. We do **not** use them to compare two things but to show that **out of three (or more)** things, **one** is of the highest or lowest degree of quality.

Warm-up

Work in pairs. Read the following conversations aloud.

CONVERSATION 1

Partner A: This was the best workshop ever!
Partner B: Yep! And the longest.
Partner A: You mean you didn't like it?
Partner B: Oh no! I loved it! Out of all the workshops, it was the most interesting one.

CONVERSATION 2

Partner A: Stella, tell me about your kids. How are they?
Partner B: They're growing up, and the three of them are surely keeping me busy.
Partner A: Are they still shy like the last time I saw them?
Partner B: Well, yes, a bit. But the youngest one, Chloe, is now the most social one.
Partner A: What about the oldest one? Is she the quietest one?
Partner B: Yes. She is the quietest and the least problematic of the three of them.

In the above conversations, what are the speakers doing?

a) They are comparing something or the person they are talking about with something or someone else.

b) They are stating that out of many things or people, this one shows the most extreme degree of quality.

In the above conversations, <u>underline</u> all the superlative adjectives. Can you guess how we form superlative adjectives?

Formation

Adjective Types	Examples	Formation	Example Sentences
one-syllable adjectives	tall	Add -est.	Xiang is **the tallest** student in our class.
one-syllable adjectives ending with an -e	nice	Add -st.	Today is **the nicest** day of my life.
one-syllable adjectives ending with a consonant-vowel-consonant	big	Double the last consonant and add -est.	Their house is **the biggest** on the street.
two-syllable adjectives ending with a consonant + y	busy	Change y to i and add -est.	York Street is **the busiest** street in this city.
two-syllable adjectives adjectives of more than two syllables	creative punctual	Insert the most or the least before the adjective.	Carl is **the most creative** artist that I know. Sam is **the least punctual** worker in our company.
irregular adjectives	good bad far (distance)	No rules; memorize those adjectives.	Water is **the best** drink to quench your thirst. This car is **the worst** car in history. My school is **the farthest** place I walk to every day.

Farthest relates to distance and *furthest* relates to degree.   **Dan's statements were the furthest from the truth.**

Insert *the* before superlative adjectives.

EXERCISE 4

Fill in the blanks with the superlative form of the adjectives in parentheses.

Carmela competes in many sports. She is _____ (athletic) person I know.

Carmela competes in many sports. She is <u>the most athletic</u> person I know.

1. The Lamborghini Veneno is _____ (**expensive**) car in the world.

2. The Trans-Canada Highway is 7,821 kilometres long. It's _____ (**long**) national highway in the world.

3. Burj Khalifa is the world's _____ (**tall**) building. It's 828 metres tall.

4. My wedding was _____ (**happy**) day of my life. It was a wonderful day.

5. Miya was married three times. Her first two husbands were very good, but her third

    husband was _____ (**good**).

COMPARATIVE AND SUPERLATIVE ADVERBS

*   Comparative adverbs tell us about the difference between how **two** people, animals, or objects do something.
*   Superlative adverbs show us that among three or more people, animals, or objects, one performance is of the highest or lowest degree.

Warm-up

Circle the letter of the correct word or phrase to complete the sentences.

1. If you want fresh food every day, buy your groceries _____
    a) once a week.
    b) more frequently than once a week.

2. You got good marks last semester, but if you want better marks next semester,

    study _____
    a) harder than last semester.
    b) the same.

3. Of all the contestants, Sally sang _____
    a) beautifully.
    b) the most beautifully.

4. Kenyan had many car accidents last year. In his whole family, he drives

_____

  a) the worst.
  b) the worse.

Sentences 1 and 2 use comparative adverbs. Can you see how we form such adverbs?

_____

Sentences 3 and 4 use superlative adverbs. Can you see how we form such adverbs?

_____

Formation

Adverb Types	Examples	Formation	Example Sentences
one-syllable adverbs	fast hard	**Comparative:** add -er. **Superlative:** add -est.	Kiefer runs **faster than** Yoko. Of all the kids, Kiefer runs **the fastest**.
adverbs of two or more syllables	slowly carefully	**Comparative:** insert *more* or *less* before the adverb. **Superlative:** insert *the most* or *the least* before the adverb.	Kim writes **more / less slowly than** Jane. Ken drives **more / less carefully than** Ben. Who writes **the most / the least slowly**? Who drives **the most / the least carefully**?
exception: *early*	early	**Comparative:** change *y* to *i* and add -er. **Superlative:** insert *the* before the adverb, change *y* to *i* and add -est.	Shannon finished the test **earlier than** Matt. Who finished the test **the earliest**?
irregular adverbs	well badly	No rules; memorize those adverbs. **Comparative:** *better*, *worse* **Superlative:** *the best*, *the worst*	Katia reads **better** in French **than** in English. I feel **worse** today **than** yesterday. Melodie did **the best** on the math test. Sandrine did **the worst** in the science class.

EXERCISE 5

Fill in the blanks with the correct comparative or superlative adverb of the words in parentheses.

1. Patrick: Hey, Tom! I guess I'm late. Sorry.

   Tom: Oh no, you're not late at all. I came a bit _____ (early) than we agreed on.

   Patrick: Really? That's good. And look, David is not here yet at all.

   Tom: He actually was here already an hour ago. He arrived _____ (early), but he didn't feel well. He called me and told me that he went home.

   Patrick: Too bad! I hope he feels _____ (well) soon.

2. Lynne: Bon appétit, Betty!

   Betty: Thank you! Are you having lunch too?

   Lynne: I already finished my lunch a couple minutes ago. I ate it _____ (fast) than usual because I still have a lot of homework to do for my science class.

   Betty: I see. By the way, how are you doing in that class? I find the class very difficult.

   Lynne: I did badly last year, but this year I think I'm doing fine. Last year's teacher didn't explain the things clearly, but this year's teacher seems to teach

   _____ (skilfully). If you find the class difficult, I can help you out.

   Betty: That's nice of you. Thanks.

3. Damian: Shawn! I was looking carefully as you were playing. Wow, man! Out of all

   the drummers I know, you play drums _____ (well).

   Shawn: Well, thanks, but I think my friend Austin plays drums _____ (well) than I do.

   Damian: Are you serious?

   Shawn: Yeah. He learned how to play drums when he was very young. He is way

   faster and plays _____ (precisely) than I do.

COMMUNICATIVE ACTIVITY 3

Conversation

Work in pairs. First, read the conversations aloud from Exercise 5. Then create similar conversations by using comparative and superlative adverbs. Act them out in front of your other classmates.

EQUATIVES

We use equatives to make a comparison between two things or actions that are equal (the same). We use both adjectives and adverbs with this structure.

Idioms are phrases that have hidden meanings. They do not mean exactly what they state.

Warm-up

Here are some idioms that compare equality. Match the numbered idioms with their lettered definitions.

Idiom

1. as easy as pie

2. as clean as a whistle

3. as blind as a bat

4. as stubborn as a mule

5. as good as gold

6. as cool as a cucumber

7. as free as a bird

8. as old as the hills

Definition

a) very calm, in control of your emotions

b) not able to see well

c) very old

d) able to do what you desire; no worries or responsibilities

e) something that you can do without difficulty

f) not dirty at all; spotless

g) well behaved

h) don't want to do what others tell you to do

Formation

To form the comparison of equality, use the following structure:

Positive: *as . . . as* = the same
Negative: *not as . . . as* = less so

> The test was **as <u>easy</u> as** the assignment.
>   adj.

> Angie walks **as <u>quickly</u> as** her mother.
>   adv.

> The test was **not as <u>easy</u> as** the assignment.
>   adj.

> Angie does not walk **as <u>quickly</u> as** her mother.
>   adv.

EXERCISE 6

Use an equative with each set of words to make a sentence. Look at the example to help you.

Biking / dangerous / mountain climbing → Biking is not as dangerous as mountain climbing.

1. Our trip to Spain last year / exciting / our trip to France in 2011

   _____

2. Girls / learn / fast / boys

   _____

3. Celeste / dresses / elegantly / Marie-France

   _____

4. Fruit / sweet / ice cream

   _____

5. Bees / hardworking / ants

   _____

BRINGING IT ALL TOGETHER

 ## COMMUNICATIVE ACTIVITY 4

Role-Plays

Work in pairs. Prepare a role-play for each of the following situations. Then perform them in front of the class.

Situation A: You are 19 years old, and you want to get married to your partner. Your dad or mom thinks you are too young for marriage. Try to persuade your parent by telling him or her how good your boyfriend or girlfriend is. Use adjectives and adverbs.

Situation B: You are at a job interview. First, the interviewer asks you to tell him or her a few of your strong points. Then, the interviewer asks you about your weak points. Answer the interviewer. Use adjectives and adverbs when possible.

COMMUNICATIVE ACTIVITY 5

Game—Guess the Action

Work in two teams. Your teacher will have two boxes: one containing papers with verbs and the other one containing papers with adverbs. A member of one team goes to the front of the class and draws one verb and one adverb out of the boxes. The student acts out the words. If his or her team makes the correct guess, they get a point. If the team can't give a correct response in 30 seconds, the other team gets a chance to make a guess and score a point.

COMMUNICATIVE ACTIVITY 6

Mini Oral Presentation

Work in pairs. Choose a topic from the list below or use your own idea. Prepare a short presentation on the topic. Try to use as many comparative and superlative adjectives and adverbs as possible. Present your mini presentation to the rest of the class.

- Compare living in the city with living in the country.
- Compare living with parents with living on your own.
- Compare being married with being single.
- Compare PCs with Mac computers.

Reading

Read the passage and answer the questions that follow.

MULTIPLE INTELLIGENCES AND LEARNING STYLES

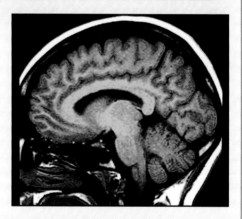

Did you know that your type of intelligence determines your learning style? A learning style is the way you learn best. People learn in different ways. For example, they learn by seeing, hearing, or doing. It's important to know what your learning style is in order to learn more <u>efficiently</u> and to get good grades. To find out what your best way of learning is, you need to know your type of intelligence. Did you know that there are eight types of intelligence, called "multiple intelligences"?

In 1983, Dr. Howard Gardner developed the theory of multiple intelligences. According to the theory, people have eight different intelligences. The type of intelligence can determine the way people process new information and learn. The following are descriptions of the eight types of intelligence and their connections to a person's learning style.

Spatial

People with <u>spatial</u> intelligence have the ability to <u>visualize</u> well with their minds. They are good at imagining, drawing, and designing. They learn quickly with visual aids.

Linguistic

People who have linguistic intelligence are good with words and languages. They learn more easily by reading, writing, listening, or discussing issues.

Logical-mathematical

People who <u>display</u> this type of intelligence are logical and rational. They like to know how things work, and they show high mathematical abilities, as well as capabilities for reasoning and scientific thinking. They learn best by asking questions, doing experiments, and solving problems.

Bodily-kinesthetic

People who have bodily-<u>kinesthetic</u> intelligence are skilful in physical activities, sports, and dance. They learn efficiently by <u>incorporating</u> movement into their learning experience.

Musical

Those with musical intelligence have a great ability to create and appreciate music, so they often sing or play a musical instrument. They learn typically by listening to lectures, music, or other audio material.

Interpersonal

People who have a high interpersonal intelligence are social, and they <u>interact</u> well with other people. They understand others easily. They learn <u>predominantly</u> by working with others in a group as they enjoy collaborative activities.

Intrapersonal

Individuals with intrapersonal intelligence know themselves very well. They have an ability to reflect on their own behaviour. They are often independent, so they learn best by studying alone.

Naturalistic

People who display naturalistic intelligence connect well with nature. They enjoy being outdoors and caring for animals and plants. They learn best in a natural environment where they can observe and relate the studied material to the world around them.

So which intelligences do you have? According to Gardner, we are born with all of the intelligences, but each of us develops a set of different types of intelligence. Therefore, you might have a few of them or even show some characteristics of each of them. Remember, you learn most efficiently if you know what your learning style is, and your learning style depends on what type or types of intelligence you have.

Adapted from Howard Gardner, M.D., *Frames of Mind*; and Sue Douglass Fliess, "Multiple Intelligences: Understanding Your Child's Learning Style."

COMPREHENSION

Answer the questions. Use complete sentences.

1. What is a learning style?

   _____

2. Why is it important to know your learning style?

   _____

3. What did Dr. Gardner develop? When was it?

   _____

4. Add the missing information in the chart below.

Type of Intelligence	The Best Way to Learn
spatial	
linguistic	
	by asking questions, _____, _____
bodily-kinesthetic	
musical	
	by working with others in a group
intrapersonal	
naturalistic	

ANALYZING THE READING PASSAGE

List ten adjectives from the reading passage.

_____

_____

List five adverbs from the reading passage.

_____

DISCUSSION

What types of intelligences do you possess? What is your best learning style? Does it correspond to the type or types of intelligence you have?

Listening

🔊 Track 13

MY FUTURE SPOUSE

Listen to the audio. You will hear three young people describe what qualities they would like their future spouse to have.

COMPREHENSION

Fill in the chart below based on what you heard.

Questions	Wendy	Simon	Eveline
What are some important qualities of a spouse?			
What is the most important quality of a spouse?			
What are the least important qualities of a spouse?			
What is an absolute no-no?			

Writing

Write a short composition (maximum 150 words) about your personality. In the first paragraph, try to describe yourself. Use as many adjectives and adverbs as possible. In the second paragraph, use the same or different adjectives to compare yourself with someone else (for example, your sibling or friend). In the last paragraph, write about what characteristics you want to develop in the future. Below are some examples of sentences, then a list of descriptive adjectives and their opposites to guide your writing.

I am an **enthusiastic** teacher, and my students tell me that I teach **well.**

Compared with my friend, I am **calmer** than she is.

In the future, I want to be **less selfish** and to help others **more frequently.**

- caring / indifferent
- considerate / inconsiderate
- disciplined / undisciplined
- flexible / stubborn
- friendly / unfriendly
- humble / arrogant
- kind / unkind

- mature / immature
- optimistic / pessimistic
- open-minded / closed-minded
- patient / impatient
- punctual / unpunctual
- respectful / disrespectful
- self-confident / insecure

CHAPTER REVIEW

Summary

- Adjectives modify nouns and pronouns.

- Adverbs modify verbs and other adverbs.

- When we compare two things, we use comparative adjectives. We form them by adding -er or *more than* or *less than.*

- When we compare the actions of two people or objects, we use comparative adverbs. We form them the same way as we form comparative adjectives.

- We use superlative adjectives when talking about three or more things. Superlative adjectives express that one thing, place, or person (out of many) is of the highest or lowest degree of quality. We form them by adding -est, or *the most* or *the least.*

- We use superlative adverbs to show that the actions of one out of many is of the highest or lowest degree. We form them the same way as we form superlative adjectives.

- We also use the equative structure "as . . . as" with adjectives and adverbs. Equatives indicate that two descriptions of adjectives or adverbs are or aren't the same.

EXERCISE 1

Fill in the blanks with either an adjective or an adverb. Use the words in parentheses.

Paper burns _____ (quick). → Paper burns <u>quickly</u>.

1. The weather was _____ (terrible) yesterday.

2. Could you please spell your name _____ (slow)?

3. This soup is _____ (delicious).

4. They lost the game because they played _____ (bad).

5. Grant speaks _____ (fast).

EXERCISE 2

Fill in the blanks with the comparative, superlative, or equative form of the adjectives or adverbs in parentheses.

1. The state of Florida is _____ (big) than England.

2. At the 2012 Olympics, Usain Bolt won a gold medal in the men's 100 metres. He

   ran _____ (fast).

3. _____ (long) word in the English language, according to the
   Oxford Dictionary of English, is pneumonoultramicroscopicsilicovolcanoconiosis.

4. Mont Blanc in Europe is not _____ (tall) as Kilimanjaro in Africa.

5. Victoria speaks Russian _____ (fluently) than English.

EXERCISE 3

There are seven adjective or adverb errors in the following passage. Find and correct them.

In 2008, Jose left his more native country, Portugal, and immigrated to Canada.
He found a lot of differences between the two countries and the people. First,
Canada was much cold than Portugal. He had to buy warmest clothes. Second,
he found that people in Canada were always walking fastly. But the bigest surprise
to him was that in the morning, on the way to work, he would see people on the
bus carrying their coffee travel mugs instead of stopping by a café and having a
nicer cup of coffee there. A year passed, and one day as Jose was going to work,
he smiled as he saw his reflection in a store window: he was in a puffy winter coat,
walking quick and holding on to his warm travel mug!

EXERCISE 4

(Circle) the letter of the correct word or phrase to complete the sentences.

1. This snowmobile is _____ that one.
   a) better
   b) as good as
   c) the best

2. The giant squid has _____ eyes in the world.
   a) the large
   b) the largest
   c) larger

3. Who is _____ student today?
   a) most tired
   b) the most tiredest
   c) the most tired

4. This lamp is _____ that one.
   a) the brightest
   b) as bright
   c) brighter than

5. Turtles are known to move very _____.
   a) slowly
   b) more slowly
   c) slow

EXERCISE 5

Unscramble the following words and make them into sentences or questions.

This / that / easier / exercise / than / one / is → **This exercise is easier than that one.**

1. than / My / neighbours / friendlier / are / yours

   _____.

2. Milos / well / cook / very / Does

   _____?

3. longest / is / river / What / in the world / the

   _____?

4. yesterday / as / Today / as / was / hot

   _____.

5. speaks / than / Hector / his son / faster

   _____.

Word Choice, Word Pairs

OVERVIEW

- Homonyms are words that sound the same but have different spellings and meanings.

- Commonly confused words sometimes sound or look similar or are sometimes mispronounced, but they have different meanings and uses.

- Certain word pairs, such as *really* and *very*, *some* and *any*, and certain prepositions often cause difficulty. Sometimes, we can use either one of the pair to mean the same thing, but in other situations, we cannot use them in the same way. The verbs *listen*, *hear*, *look*, *see*, and *watch* sometimes cause confusion. The meanings of the verbs change when there is a preposition after them.

Warm-up

Work in pairs. Read the following sentences. Focus on the words **in bold**.

You're here to hear the **two** bands play, aren't you? Are **your** friends **here too**?

We **live** near the Arts Centre, and we **really** enjoy going to concerts there to **listen to live** music. We also like to **watch** films in the IMAX theatre **very** much.

Now listen to your teacher read the sentences. What do you think is the same and what is different about those words? In the first two sentences, what are the pairs of words that sound the same? What do you think the difference is between them? Identify the pairs of words in the third sentence. What do you think the difference is between them?

HOMONYMS AND COMMONLY CONFUSED WORDS

Homonyms are pairs or groups of words that sound the same, but their spelling and their meanings are different.

Commonly confused words look or sound a little similar, or they are sometimes pronounced incorrectly, but their meanings and uses are different.

Warm-up

Listen to your teacher read the following sentences. Are the words **in bold** in each sentence pronounced the same way? What do you think is the difference between them?

1. The **two** boys want **to** go **to** the party **too**.

2. **His** sister **is** in **their** house, but **he's** over **there**.

3. **You're** not angry with **your** brother. **You're** angry with **your** sister.

4. The dog is chasing **its** tail. **It's** funny.

HOMONYMS

Formation

Form	Meaning and Use	Example Sentences
it's	*It's* is the contracted or short form for *it is* and *it has*.	**It's** a beautiful day today.
its	*Its* is the possessive adjective and pronoun for the third-person singular (for things and animals, never people).	Look at this flower and **its** colour!
you're	*You're* is the contracted or short form for *you are*.	**You're** visiting **your** sister.
your	*Your* is the possessive adjective for the second-person singular and plural (for people only).	
they're	*They're* is the contracted or short form for *they are*.	**They're** doing **their** homework in the classroom over **there**.
their	*Their* is the possessive adjective for the third-person plural (for people, things, and animals).	
there	We use *there* + *be* to introduce the existence of something or someone.	**There** are a lot of students in the classroom.
	There is also an adverb of place (away from this place).	Where is your car? It's over **there**.
hear	*Hear* is a verb. It's the action you do with your ears. (*Ear* is in the word *hear*.)	I **hear** a dog barking near **here**.
here	We use *here* + *be* to present something or someone.	**Here** is your book.
	Here is also an adverb of place (in this place).	I'll put it **here** on the desk.

Continued

TIP FOR USING *THEY'RE, YOU'RE, AND IT'S*

If the word has an apostrophe, rewrite the word as two words. Is it still correct?

> **They're** at home. →
> **They are** at home.

TIP FOR USING *THEIR, YOUR, AND ITS*

If the word seems to be a possessive form, check if there is a noun following it. Replace it with a different possessive adjective. Is it still correct?

> **Their** book is there. →
> **Your** book is there.

TIPS FOR USING *THERE* AND *HERE*

If the word is referring to place, replace it with another adverb or phrase that refers to place. Is it still correct?

> Their book is **there**. → Their book is **here (on the table)**.

Always check the words that follow. Do you need to add a verb or is it already there?

> **There** <u>is</u> a book over **there**.

TIPS FOR USING *TO*, *TOO*, AND *TWO*

Check the words after *to*. *To* can come before a verb, a noun, or a pronoun.

> I want **to** go **to** the movies.

If you see the words *much* or *many*, you need to use *too*, not *to* or *two*, before them.

> I can't go to the movies because I have **too** much homework to do.

Replace *too* with *also*. Is it still correct?

> I enjoy going to the movies **too**.
> → I enjoy going to the movies **also**.

Replace *two* with another number. Is it still correct?

> I have **two** brothers. →
> I have **three** brothers.

TIPS FOR USING *ONE* AND *WON*

Replace *one* with another number. Is it still correct?

> I have **one** dollar. →
> I have **two** dollars.

Replace *won* with *lost*, the past tense of *lose*. Is it still correct?

> I **won** 10 dollars. →
> I **lost** 10 dollars.

Form	Meaning and Use	Example Sentences
to	*To* is a preposition. We use it • with the infinitive of a verb. • with an indirect object. • to show direction.	Jean needs **to** work. Please give it **to** me. Let's go **to** the park. I want **to** go **to** the store **to** buy a gift **to** give **to** Julia.
too	*Too* is an adverb. It emphasizes or intensifies the word it is modifying. Sometimes, *too* means *also*. It usually comes at the end of a sentence.	We have **too** many things to do today. They want to go swimming **too**.
two	*Two* is the number 2. *Two* can come before a plural noun or appear on its own.	I have **two** assignments **to** do **too**.
one	*One* is the number 1. *One* can come before a singular noun or appear on its own.	I have two cookies. Would you like **one**?
won	*Won* is the simple past tense of the verb to *win*.	My friend **won** the writing competition.

EXERCISE 1

Circle the correct word in the parentheses to complete each sentence.

1. Are (**they're / their / there**) many books in the library? Yes. (**It's / Its**) great to have a lot of variety when (**you're / your**) doing research for school projects. I sometimes go (**to / too / two**) the library (**to / too**

/ **two**) borrow audio books. (**They're / Their / There**) is a pretty good selection of those (**to / too / two**).

2. Did you (**hear / here**) that loud noise coming from the next room? What do you think they were doing in (**they're / their / there**)? I don't know, but it was certainly loud in (**hear / here**).

3. Sylvain and I each (**one / won**) a prize at the party. I chose a DVD. Sylvain got a different (**one / won**).

EXERCISE 2

Fill in the blanks to correctly complete the sentences. Use words from the list. Not all the words are used.

it's / its
your / you're
they're / their / there
hear / here
to / too / two

1. Please put the keys on the counter over _____.

2. Please turn up the volume. It's _____ quiet. I want

    to _____ the broadcast of the New Year's Eve show

    _____.

3. Is that Marco's new car? Wow, _____ great!

4. The teacher asked the students to bring _____ books to class.

5. Please come _____. I want to look at _____
    ring more closely.

EXERCISE 3

There are five word choice errors in the following paragraph. Find and correct them.

My friend Vladimir has a big family. Their are five boys and two girls. They live in
a house on you're street. Do you want to go by his house to see if he wants to go
too play street hockey with us? Its not far from hear.

 # COMMUNICATIVE ACTIVITY 1

Creative Sentences

Work in pairs. Together write one sentence for each of the homonyms in the Formation
chart on pages 127–128. Then try to write one sentence that includes all homonyms in
each group. Compare your sentences with another pair's sentences.

Here is my book.

I **hear** the phone ringing.

Do you **hear** the neighbours talking from in **here**?

TIP FOR USING *AS* AND *HAS*

Change the person and replace *has* with *have* or another verb. Is it still correct?

He has a twin brother. →
I have a twin brother.

TIPS FOR USING *IS*, *HIS*, AND *HE'S*

Change the person and replace *is* with *am* or *are*. Is it still correct?

The dog is in the kitchen. →
The dogs are in the kitchen.

Replace *his* with a different possessive adjective. Is it still correct?

His car is in the garage. →
My car is in the garage.

Rewrite the word *he's* as two words. Is it still correct?

He's busy. → **He is** busy.

TIPS FOR USING *LIVE*, *LIFE*, AND *LEAVE*

Change the person to *he, she*, or *it,* and replace *live* with *lives*. Is it still correct?

I live in Ontario. →
He lives in Ontario.

Replace *live* with another adjective. Is it still correct?

We enjoy **live** performances. →
We enjoy **beautiful** performances.

Continued

COMMONLY CONFUSED WORDS

Formation

Form	Meaning and Use	Example Sentences
as	*As* introduces equality. *As* can come before <ul><li>an adjective.</li><li>an adverb.</li><li>a subject and verb.</li></ul>There is no /h/ sound at the beginning.	It's **as** cold **as** ice. He moves **as** slowly **as** a snail. You take the same bus **as** I take.
has	*Has* is a simple present form of the verb *have*. *Has* comes after a singular noun or a subject pronoun (*he, she, it*). It has an /h/ sound at the beginning.	He **has** the same class schedule **as** I do.
is	*Is* is a simple present form of the verb *be*. *Is* comes after a singular noun, a subject pronoun (*he, she, it*), or a question word.	Franz **is** my friend. It **is** late. What **is** her address?
his	*His* is the possessive adjective and pronoun for the third-person singular (for male people only).	He trims **his** beard every morning.
he's	*He's* has an apostrophe, so it is the contracted or short form of *he is*.	**He's** from Guatemala. **He's** my friend and **his** name **is** Sergio.
live	*Live* is the verb that means to have life. *Live* has the short /i/ sound and comes after a noun or a subject pronoun.	We **live** in Ottawa. Franklin **lives** with his family.
	Live (with a long /i/ sound as in *life*) describes an activity as it is happening.	The program is streaming **live** on the Internet. It's a **live** broadcast.
life	*Life* is a noun that means the time from birth to death or existence. (*Lives* is the plural form.)	The **life** of a student is often difficult and fun at the same time.
leave	*Leave* is the verb that means to go away from a place. *Leave* comes after a noun or a subject pronoun.	The train **leaves** at 9:15.

Continued

Form	Meaning and Use	Example Sentences
where	*Where* is a pronoun that refers to a place.	**Where** do you live?
were	*Were* is a simple past tense form of the verb *be*.	You **were** sad yesterday. We **were** at the college on the weekend. They **were** in the swimming pool all day. **Where were** the boys yesterday at 7:00 PM?
than	We use *than* to compare people and things (see Chapter 7).	I like strawberries more **than** apples.
then	*Then* refers to a time in the past or it introduces the next thing or action in a series.	He was at home **then** (at that time). I want to finish my work first. **Then** I want to go to the movies.

EXERCISE 4

Fill in the blanks to correctly complete the sentences. Use words from the list. Not all the words are used.

as / has
is / his / he's
lives / life / leave
where / were
than / then

1. _____ was Jim when the storm started? _____ not

   answering _____ cellphone. He usually _____ it on

   all the time. I'm beginning to worry about him.

2. My brother _____ three years younger _____ I am.

   He still _____ at home with our parents. He _____

   one more year of high school to finish; _____ he's going to

   _____ our town to go to university in another city.

Check the words before and after *life*. For example, is there an article or adjective before *life* or a verb or another phrase after it?

The **life** of a politician must be very stressful.

I enjoy my **life**.

Scientists are always looking for signs of **life** in outer space.

Change the person to *he, she*, or *it,* and replace *leave* with *leaves*. Is it still correct? Be careful! *Leaves* is also the plural of the noun *leaf*.

I often **leave** for school at 7:00 AM. → He often **leaves** for school at 7:00 AM.

TIPS FOR USING *WHERE* AND *WERE*

Always check the words that follow. Is the word a pronoun or part of a verb? Do you need to add a verb or is it already there?

I don't know **where** it is. **Where were** you last night? We **were** at the movies.

TIP FOR USING *THAN* AND *THEN*

Replace the word *than* or *then* with *at that time* or *next*. Is it still correct?

I have more fun at school **than** at work. (Using *at that time* or *next* doesn't make sense.)

I knew him **then**. → I knew him **at that time**.

I go to work for five hours; **then** I go home. → I go to work for five hours; **next** I go home.

WORD PAIRS

Certain word pairs cause difficulty because we can use them similarly in some cases but not in others.

Warm-up

Work in pairs. Read the following sentences, and focus on the words **in bold**.

1. You were **going home** while I was **going to** work. Now you're **at** home and I'm **at** work.

2. When the teacher walked **into** the room, Jorge was already **in** there.

3. She made the cake **from** scratch. The cake pan is made **of** aluminum.

How are the pairs of words different? Is there a difference in their meaning?

Formation

Form	Meaning and Use	Example Sentences
really very	*Really* and *very* are both adverbs that have the same meaning. They both intensify the meaning of the adjective or adverb they come before. However, only *really* can modify a verb and only *very* can modify *much*.	Your friend is **really** nice. Your friend is **very** nice. I **really** like to play basketball. He likes to watch soccer on TV **very** much.
some any	*Some* and *any* introduce non-countable nouns and nouns with indefinite quantities. (We don't know how much or how many things there are.) We use *some* in positive sentences. We use *any* in questions and in negatives.	I have **some** money. He has **some** visitors this weekend. I have **some** money in my wallet. Do you have **any** money? He doesn't have **any** visitors this weekend.
no not any	*No* and *not any* show the absence or lack of something. Remember that in English, there can only be **one negative signal**. For example, you can say "no" or "not any," but you cannot say "not no."	I have **no** energy today. (correct) I **don't** have **any** energy today. (correct) I **don't** have **no** energy today. (incorrect)

Form	Meaning and Use	Example Sentences
to	*To* indicates a direction, some movement, and an end location.	Tran drives **to** Montreal every Friday. (movement and a destination)
at	*At* presents a specific location.	Frank is sitting **at** his desk. We are **at** home, and he is **at** school. (no movement, a specific location)
	With the verb *go*, *to* usually comes before the destination, except with *home*.	I **go to** work on Monday morning. I **go home** after work.
from	*From* gives the origin of someone or something or tells how something was made.	Yuliya is **from** Russia. This sweater is made **from** wool.
of	*Of* gives us information about the original material of a thing.	This purse is made **of** leather. The desk is made **of** wood.
for	*For* indicates a quantity of time.	He lived in Germany **for** three years. **During** that time, he worked at the university in Hamburg.
during	*During* indicates the period of time.	High school students are on holidays **for** nine weeks **during** the summer.
in	*In* refers to something that is static (not changing place). It means that someone or something is inside some space.	The students are **in** the classroom.
into	*Into* gives the idea of movement or going inside some space.	The doctor came **into** the patient's room. (This sentence has movement.)
on	*On* is also static, and it means that someone or something is on the surface of something else.	The suitcases are **on** the station platform.
onto	*Onto* gives the idea of movement to the top of that surface.	The passenger stepped off the train and **onto** the platform. (This sentence has movement.)

EXERCISE 5

Fill in the blanks to correctly complete the sentences. Use the words from the list. Use each word only once.

any	during	really	to	very	in	at	from	on	for

1. I studied Spanish _____ two months.

2. Sanda enjoys dancing _____ much.

3. Please put it _____ the kitchen counter.

4. Hank is _____ Winnipeg.

5. I think your glasses are _____ the desk drawer.

6. I don't have _____ money.

7. We are going _____ the gallery.

8. They didn't know each other _____ that time.

9. I was _____ school today.

10. Maria _____ enjoyed her trip to Australia.

COMMUNICATIVE ACTIVITY 2

Concentration Game

Work in small groups. Your teacher will give each group two sets of cards. One set has sentences with a missing word. The other set has the missing words. Shuffle both sets. Place the cards of one set face down on the left side of the desk. Place the other cards face down on the right side. Take turns revealing one card from the left group and one card from the right. The object is to match the sentence with its missing word. If there is no match, turn the cards face down again, and try to remember what words were on the cards. If there is a match, set the pair aside. The player in each group with the most matched pairs wins, and the team to finish first also wins.

LISTEN, HEAR, LOOK, SEE, WATCH

The meanings of the verbs *listen*, *hear*, *look*, *see*, and *watch* are often confusing. Also, the meanings of the verbs change when there is a preposition after them.

Warm-up

Work in pairs. Read the following sentences, and focus on the words in **bold**.

When I **listen to** music on the radio, I often **hear** new information about the musicians.
When you **look at** a painting, what do you **see**?
When you **are watching** people in the park, what do you **see**?

What do you think is the difference in meaning between the pairs of verbs?

Formation

Form	Meaning and Use	Example Sentences
hear	To *hear* is the ability to perceive sound with your ears. (*Hear* is often followed by *about*.)	I **hear** children laughing in the park. (physical ability) I **heard** about your promotion. Congratulations! (message received and understood)
listen to	To *listen* is to actively or purposely pay attention to what you hear. Listen is always followed by *to*.	I always **listen to** the radio on my way to work. (actively paying attention)
see	To *see* is the ability to see with your eyes.	I **see** birds in the trees. (physical ability)
look at	To *look at* is to purposely see a fixed scene.	She is **looking** at her watch. (a fixed look)
watch	To *watch* involves purposely seeing and observing action or movement.	We **watched** TV last night. (observing the action)
look for	To *look for* means to search for something that is missing or cannot be seen.	I'm **looking for** my keys. I can't find them.
watch for	We use *watch for* when someone expects something is going to happen.	He is **watching** the clouds in the sky **for** signs of a storm coming.
look out	To *look out* means you are inside looking at a scene outside.	I was **looking out** the window when I saw him.
watch out	It also means a warning to be careful.	**Watch out**! (Look out!) There's a car coming.

EXERCISE 6

Circle the correct words in the parentheses to complete each sentence.

1. My family enjoys (**listening to / looking at / watching**) movies in the evening.

2. What are you (**looking / seeing / watching**) at?

3. Did you (**hear / listen to**) someone at the door?

4. John (**was looking for / was looking at / was watching for**) his glasses, but they were on his head.

5. Look (**at / for / out**)! The sign says "wet paint."

BRINGING IT ALL TOGETHER

 ## COMMUNICATIVE ACTIVITY 3

Spelling Bee

Work in two teams. Your teacher will read a short sentence and repeat the word you need to spell. A member of Team A writes the correct spelling of the word on the board. If the answer is correct, that team scores a point. If not, Team B gets a chance to spell it correctly and steal a point. Your teacher will then read another sentence and word for Team B. The team with the most points wins.

 ## COMMUNICATIVE ACTIVITY 4

Scrambled Sentences

Work in teams of three or four. Your teacher will give your group five sets of cards. Each set has all the parts of a sentence. The objective is to put the sentences together in the correct order. The team that finishes first wins.

Reading

Read the passage and answer the questions that follow.

THE ENGLISH LANGUAGE

Languages <u>constantly</u> <u>evolve</u> and change, especially with the <u>influences</u> of other languages. The English language is no exception. Old English had a large vocabulary, but many of the more common words were short one-syllable words like *hard*, *go*, or *get*. However, there were many influences on the language as it continued to develop. For example, the names of the days of the week have Norse and Anglo-Saxon beginnings. *Thursday* comes from the name of the Norse god Thor. The Romans and the French had a big influence on the development of the English language too. Their major influence happened during the periods in history when England was under their control. Then English had its turn to be an influence. In fact, the spread of the English language has its <u>roots</u> in the <u>colonization</u> of the countries <u>conquered</u> by the British Empire.

English continues to <u>expand</u> its influence today. Mandarin Chinese, Spanish, and English are the three most commonly spoken languages in the world. Although English is third, it is becoming a *lingua franca* (a universal or shared language). In fact, today, more people speak English as a second language than as their first language.

The English language also continues to expand. We are constantly creating new words and <u>adopting</u> others from foreign languages. As a result, there is no accurate count of the number of words currently used in English, but many experts think it's more than one million. With so many words, and in particular so many influences from other languages, it's no wonder that there are some confusing words and uses of words in English.

ANALYZING THE READING PASSAGE

Read the passage again. <u>Underline</u> the commonly confused words studied in this chapter. Seventeen of them are used at least once.

COMPREHENSION

Answer the questions. Use complete sentences.

1. What are three examples of Old English words?

   _____

2. Where does the word *Thursday* come from?

   _____

3. How did the English language spread?

   _____

4. What is a *lingua franca*?

   _____

5. People create new words. In what other way do we add new words to the English language?

   _____

6. Approximately how many words are there in the English language?

   _____

DISCUSSION

Other languages influenced English vocabulary, and English influenced other languages' vocabularies. Do you think that is the same for other languages? Does your first language contain words from other languages? Is it a good thing that languages adopt new words from other languages?

Listening

◀)) Track 14

Listen to the song. In the song lyrics on the next page, fill in the blanks with the words you hear.

WHAT A WONDERFUL WORLD

by George David Weiss, George Douglas, and Bob Thiele

I see trees of green, red roses _____

I _____ them bloom for me and you

And I think to myself what a wonderful world.

I _____ skies of blue and clouds of white

The bright blessed day, the dark sacred night

And I _____ to myself what a wonderful world.

The colors of the rainbow so pretty in the sky

Are _____ on the faces of people going by

I _____ friends shaking hands saying how do you do

They're _____ saying I love you.

I _____ babies crying, I _____ them grow

They'll learn much more _____ I'll never know

And I think to myself what a wonderful world

Yes I think to myself what a wonderful world.

COMPREHENSION

Listen to the song again. Answer the questions.

1. Why do trees, flowers, blue skies, and white clouds make this a wonderful world?

   _____

2. What does it mean that the colours of the rainbow are on the faces of the people?

   _____

3. Why does "friends shaking hands" mean the same thing as "saying I love you"?

   _____

4. Why does watching babies grow make this a wonderful world?

   _____

DISCUSSION

Listen to the song again. What do you think it's about? How does it make you feel?

Writing

Work in small groups. Your teacher will give each group a starting sentence. Each person in the group adds two sentences to create a complete story. Try to use as many of the words from this chapter as possible. Share your short stories with the other groups.

CHAPTER REVIEW

Summary

- People sometimes confuse homonyms because the words sound the same, but we spell and use them differently.

- Commonly confused words, such as *where* and *were*, are words that look or sound similar or are sometimes mispronounced but have different spellings and meanings.

- Certain word pairs, such as *really* and *very* and *to* and *at*, cause confusion because we can use them in a similar way in some situations but not in others.

- Some verbs, such as *listen*, *hear*, *look*, *see*, and *watch*, have close but different meanings. Also, the meanings of the verbs changes with different prepositions.

EXERCISE 1

Circle the correct word in parentheses to complete the sentences.

1. I like (**you're / your**) new apartment (**really / very**) much.

2. When I (**look / see / watch**) the first flower bloom (**in / into**) the spring, I feel really happy.

3. First, they went to visit (**they're / their / there**) friends. (**Than / Then**) they went shopping.

4. Carlos's team (**one / won**) the championship game. (**It's / Its**) the first time ever.

5. Didn't you (**hear / listen**) what the teacher said? You weren't (**hearing / listening**), as usual.

EXERCISE 2

There are five word choice errors in the following paragraph. Find and correct them.

I don't have some idea what to get Suzanne and Zara for there new apartment. I know they very enjoy plants. Do you think buying a nice flowering won for them is a good idea? Their also fond of music. What do you think?

EXERCISE 3

Circle the letter of the correct word or phrase to complete the sentences.

1. When does your flight _____?

     a) live   b) life   c) leave

2. Mohammad is from Iran. _____ in my English class.

     a) Is   b) He's   c) His

3. Do you know _____ Marie lives?

     a) were   b) we're   c) where

4. We have classes _____ four hours in a row.

     a) during   b) for   c) from

5. Gina _____ a new car.

     a) as   b) has   c) his

EXERCISE 4

Fill in the blanks to correctly complete the sentences. Use the words from the list. Use each word only once.

looking	of	really	too	watch	in	at	to	hear	here

1. _____ out! That chair is broken.

2. That costs _____ much.

3. The glasses are _____ the kitchen.

4. This dress is made _____ cotton.

5. That blouse is _____ pretty.

6. I like _____ at photos.

7. Put it _____ (in this place).

8. Did you _____ that noise?

9. I went _____ school today.

10. He's _____ home.

Part 2 Review

Self-Study

OVERVIEW

The self-assessments in this unit give you a chance to review and reinforce the grammar points from Part 2 (Chapters 5–8).

Check your knowledge and if you find areas that need more attention, go back to the appropriate chapter and review the material.

EXERCISE 1

Unscramble the following words and make them into sentences or questions.

it / When / happen / did → **When did it happen?**

1. more / This flower / than / beautiful / that flower / is

   _____.

2. were / Where / this morning / they

   _____?

3. really / I / comedies / love

   _____.

4. the test / well / The students / on / did

   _____.

5. new / you / any / have / Do / ideas

   _____?

6. to / you're / your / Now / going / class

   _____.

7. she / study / for / too /Did / hours / two

   _____?

8. was / Ursula / when / her husband / cooking / came back

   _____.

9. likes / music / Joshua / to / rock / listen to

   _____.

10. class / the / person / Sarah / interesting / in / most / our / is

   _____.

EXERCISE 2

Change each of the following positive sentences into the negative.

We went to Greece last summer. → **We did not go to Greece last summer.**

1. It rained heavily last night.

   _____

2. I was checking my emails yesterday between seven and eight o'clock.

   _____

3. Our biology project is as good as yours.

   _____

4. Carol won the competition.

   _____

5. The musicians were great.

   _____

EXERCISE 3

Change each of the following sentences into a yes / no question.

I was yawning when she was talking. → **Were you yawning when she was talking?**

1. They were clapping while others were singing a song.

   _____?

2. Samantha moved to Miami two years ago.

   _____?

3. Mona and Ted had a wedding anniversary party last weekend.

   _____?

4. He was eating an apple when his tooth fell out.

   _____?

5. My parents-in-law were happy to come for a visit last summer.

   _____?

EXERCISE 4

Change each of the following statements into a wh- question. The information you want to ask about is **in bold**.

You submitted the essay late. → What did you submit late?

1. The game tug-of-war became an official event **at the second modern Olympic Games** in 1900.

   _____?

2. In 1945, the first Slinky toys were **one dollar** each.

   _____?

3. In 1969, Neil Armstrong was famous **because he was the first person to set foot on the moon**.

   _____?

4. The first Ford cars had **Dodge** engines.

   _____?

5. George Stanley and John Matheson designed **the flag of Canada** in 1965.

   _____?

EXERCISE 5

Fill in the blanks with the correct form of the verbs in parentheses. Use the past progressive or simple past. Look at the example to help you.

Sergio: Do you remember that I _____ (lose) my car keys yesterday morning?

I finally _____ (find) them later on that day!

Manuel: Where _____ they (be)?

Sergio: While I _____ (get) my jeans ready for laundry, they _____ (fall) out of the pocket.

Sergio: Do you remember that I <u>lost</u> my car keys yesterday morning? I finally <u>found</u> them later on that day!

Manuel: Where <u>were</u> they?

Sergio: While I <u>was getting</u> my jeans ready for laundry, they <u>fell</u> out of the pocket.

Amy: What ₁ _____ (**happen**) to you yesterday? ₂ _____ you

_____ (**forget**) about our project meeting at five o'clock?

Brianna: What? Oh, no! I totally ₃ ——————— (forget). Sorry.

Amy: But I ₄ ——————— (call) you three times between 5:15 and 6 o'clock. What ₅ ——————— you ——————— (do)?

Brianna: I ₆ ——————— (be) tired, so I ₇ ——————— (sleep). I ₈ ——————— (hear, negative) the phone. ₉ ——————— you ——————— (start) the project without me?

Amy: No way! I ₁₀ ——————— (want, negative) to start it all by myself. It's a team project.

Brianna: You're right. Let's meet tomorrow.

EXERCISE 6

Unscramble the following words and make them into sentences or questions.

This / that / easier / exercise / than / one / is → This exercise is easier than that one.

1. than / My / neighbours / friendlier / are / yours

   _____.

2. Milos / well / cook / very / Does

   _____?

3. longest / is / river / What / in the world / the

   _____?

4. yesterday / as / Today / as / was / hot

   _____.

5. speaks / than / Hector / his son / faster

   _____.

EXERCISE 7

Correct the errors in the following sentences. The errors are <u>underlined</u>.

1. She <u>studyed</u> for the test all weekend long.

2. We were sleeping <u>while</u> the phone rang.

3. He always took time to <u>watch</u> my paintings and to give me feedback.

4. <u>Reds</u> apples are sweeter than green apples.

5. I was <u>waiting Abdul</u> when you called me on my cellphone.

6. Yesterday, I bought <u>too</u> sweaters, not one.

7. Both drivers <u>was</u> speeding.

8. He was dancing with <u>he's</u> girlfriend when he tripped and fell.

9. I don't have <u>no</u> money.

10. When did he <u>live</u> the hotel?

11. The store closed earlier <u>then</u> usual.

12. <u>Were</u> are the kids?

13. I didn't <u>worked</u> at the university in 2009.

14. The weather was <u>badder</u> yesterday than it is today.

15. They <u>bringed</u> many souvenirs from their trip to Nova Scotia.

16. Hiroko is <u>least competitive</u> child in our family.

17. The tongue is <u>the most strong</u> muscle in the human body.

18. <u>Its</u> a very pretty necklace.

19. <u>Their</u> are 20 students in my chemistry class.

20. Vanilla ice cream is as <u>yummier</u> as chocolate ice cream.

Simple Future— *Will* and *Be Going To*

OVERVIEW

In English, there are two main verb formations to express future plans and actions: *will* and *be going to*.

Use	Form	Keywords	Example Sentences
spontaneous, voluntary, or probable actions, predictions	*will* + verb	later on today soon **this** week / year / Sunday in the morning / afternoon tomorrow **next** weekend / week / year / summer / vacation / holiday	I **will study** later. You **will have** good marks. He **will come** tomorrow. It **will rain** today. We **will invite** them. They **will help** us next week.
planned future actions, predictions	*be going to* + verb	in the future in five years on June 15 (specific date) in 2012 (specific year) **when** I get home . . . **after** he finishes school . . .	I **am going to make** dinner tonight. You **are going to graduate** in two years. She **is going to study** in Canada this year. It **is going to rain** soon. We **are going to leave** at five o'clock. They **are going to call** us when they get there.

Warm-up

Create a survey chart like the one below. Walk around the classroom. Ask three of your classmates the questions, and record their answers.

Name	Tonight	Next Weekend	After You Graduate
	What are your plans for tonight?	What are your plans for next weekend?	What are your plans after you graduate?

WILL

One of the verb formations to express a future action is with *will*. We use this form for spontaneous and voluntary actions and predictions.

At the end of high school, students get a yearbook. This book consists of photos of students, teachers, and different activities that took place over the last year of high school. It's an annual tradition for graduating students to submit a few final words of wisdom to go along with their senior portraits. Some students also include their future plans, especially about who they want to be in the future.

Warm-up

Work in pairs. Look at the yearbook photos of the graduating high school students and the descriptions next to each photo. Use the information to form complete sentences about these students' futures.

1. Name: Yoshi Kuma

   Plans: go to university, move to another country

   Future profession: businessperson

2. Name: Emilia Smith

   Plans: have lots of kids

   Future profession: stay-at-home mom or kindergarten teacher

3. Name: Mat Sanders

   Plans: open an auto-body shop, fix cars

   Future profession: a car mechanic or a car designer

4. Name: Hoda Miseri

    Plans: travel a lot

    Future profession: journalist

Formation

Positive	Negative	Question	Wh- Question
Subject + Auxiliary + Verb (+ object / complement)	Subject + Auxiliary + Negative + Verb (+ object / complement)	Auxiliary + Subject + Verb (+ object / complement)	Question Word + Auxiliary + Subject + Verb (+ object / complement)
I **will** do it now.	I **will not** do it now.	**Will** you do it now?	**Why** will you do it now?
You **will** get this job.	You **will not** get this job.	**Will** you get this job?	**How** will you get this job?
He **will** get better soon.	He **will not** get better soon.	**Will** he get better soon?	**When** will he get better?
She **will** have the best marks.	She **will not** have the best marks.	**Will** she have the best marks?	**What** marks will she have?
It **will** be sunny tomorrow.	It **will not** be sunny tomorrow.	**Will** it be sunny tomorrow?	**How** will it be tomorrow?
We **will** keep in touch.	We **will not** keep in touch.	**Will** we keep in touch?	**How** will we keep in touch?
They **will** travel this summer.	They **will not** travel this summer.	**Will** they travel this summer?	**When** will they travel?

Note: For a detailed explanation of how to form and use questions and negatives, refer to Chapter 11.

- *Will* is an auxiliary.
- The contracted forms of the subject + *will* are *I'll*, *you'll*, *she'll*, *he'll*, *we'll*, and *they'll*.
- The negative contracted form of *will* + *not* is *won't*.

EXERCISE 1

Fill in the blanks with *will* and the correct form of the verbs in parentheses.

He decided that he _____ (become) a computer programmer.

He decided that he <u>will become</u> a computer programmer.

1. Marianna is tired tonight, so she _____ (do) homework tomorrow.

2. _____ it _____ (be) windy this weekend?

3. They _____ (stay, not) for long.

4. We _____ (miss) you.

5. _____ you _____ (call) me later?

EXERCISE 2

Change each of the following sentences into a yes / no question.

They will take the train. → **Will they take the train?**

1. The plane will depart at noon.

   _____?

2. Theodora will pay her phone bill next week.

   _____?

3. We'll see you tomorrow.

   _____?

4. I will go to bed late.

   _____?

5. Joan's brother will answer that question.

   _____?

✦ COMMUNICATIVE ACTIVITY 1

News from the Future

Work in small groups. Read the following magazine articles from the future. Below each article, rewrite it. Change the sentences that have any other verb tenses to sentences that express the future with *will*. Make all other necessary changes. To help you, the possible changes are <u>underlined</u>. The first article is done for you.

First Hotel on the Moon Finally Opens
August 23, 2025—<u>Today</u>, a new chapter in space tourism <u>was</u> written. Rod Markham and his wife-to-be, Susan Millster, <u>arrived</u> safely on the moon to spend five days as the first guests at the Starbright Hotel, which <u>was</u> set up for this purpose <u>two years ago</u>. They <u>are not</u> only the first hotel guests on the moon, but they <u>also set</u> a new record for most-expensive accommodation since the price <u>was</u> US$3.7 million per night, per person. However, the exclusive transfer from earth to the hotel <u>was</u> included in the price.

On August 23, 2025, a new chapter in space tourism **will be** written. Rod Markham and his wife-to-be, Susan Millster, **will arrive** safely on the moon to spend five days as the first guests at the Starbright Hotel. The hotel **will be** set up for this purpose **in 2023**. They **will not only be** the first hotel guests on the moon, but they **will also set** a new record for most-expensive accommodation since the price **will be** US$3.7 million per night, per person. However, the exclusive transfer from earth to the hotel **will be** included in the price.

1. Icelandic Hydrogen Finally Pushed Gasoline off the Road

   November 19, 2040—<u>Today</u> <u>was</u> a historic day for Iceland when its president at a symbolic ceremony officially <u>shut</u> down the last gasoline pump in the country. Iceland <u>is</u> a model country when it comes to the fuel transition from gasoline to hydrogen, and it <u>became</u> <u>today</u> the first country in the world to complete it.

   _____

   _____

   _____

   _____

   _____

   _____

   _____

   _____

2. Do the Anti-Aging Drugs Work?

   March 20, 2035—There <u>was</u> a lot of buzz around the life extension drugs that <u>hit</u> the market <u>a decade ago</u>. They <u>didn't promise</u> you a life forever, but they <u>gave</u> you a chance to maybe extend your life with an extra five to ten years. But <u>do</u> they work?

   _____

   _____

   _____

   _____

   _____

   _____

   _____

   _____

Adapted from News of the Future website at www.newsoffuture.com.

BE GOING TO

We use the form *be going to* to express a future action that is already planned. We also use this form to make predictions.

Warm-up

Work in pairs. Look at the following pictures. Finish the sentence underneath each picture.

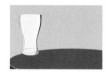

1. Tonight, it _____

2. Tomorrow _____

3. It was cold this week, but this weekend _____

4. Look out! That glass _____

5. Henry is ready. He _____

Formation

Positive	Negative	Question	Wh- Question
Subject + *be* + *Going to* + Verb (+ object / complement)	Subject + *be* + Negative + *Going to* + Verb (+ object / complement)	*Be* + Subject + *Going to* + Verb (+ object / complement)	Question Word + *be* + Subject + *Going to* + Verb (+ object / complement)
I **am going to** speak with her.	I **am not going to** speak with her.	**Are** you **going to** speak with her?	**Who** are you going to speak with?
You **are going to** pass this course.	You **are not going to** pass this course.	**Are** you **going to** pass this course?	**How** are you going to pass this course?

Positive	Negative	Question	Wh- Question
He **is going to** be 18 years old next week.	He **is not going to** be 18 years old next week.	**Is** he **going to** be 18 years old next week?	**How old** is he going to be next week?
She **is going to** travel to Asia this summer.	She **is not going to** travel to Asia this summer.	**Is** she **going to** travel to Asia this summer?	**Where** is she going to travel this summer?
It **is going to** snow tomorrow.	It **is not going to** snow tomorrow.	**Is** it **going to** snow tomorrow?	**When** is it going to snow?
We **are going to** buy a new house in two years.	We **are not going to** buy a new house in two years.	**Are** we **going to** buy a new house in two years?	**What** are we going to buy in two years?
They **are going to** leave soon.	They **are not going to** leave soon.	**Are** they **going to** leave soon?	**When** are they going to leave?

Remember: The verb *be* does not need an auxiliary verb in negatives or questions.

EXERCISE 3

Read each sentence and determine if it expresses a plan or a prediction.

After class, I am going to go home.   plan

My husband is going to be well-known one day.   prediction

1. I'm hungry. I'm going to make myself a sandwich. _____

2. Stan is very sick today. He is going to stay home tomorrow. _____

3. The sky is grey. It's going to rain. _____

4. Next year, my daughter is going to join the gymnastics team. _____

5. Luke and Carmen are in love. I think they are going to get married. _____

EXERCISE 4

Fill in the blanks with *be going to* and the correct form of the verbs in parentheses.

Shaun _____ (watch) TV tonight.   →   Shaun <u>is going to watch</u> TV tonight.

1. You _____ (have) a quiz tomorrow morning.

2. _____ we _____ (do) a group project this semester?

3. Abdul _____ (move, not) to Canada.

4. _____ the course notes _____ (be) available online?

5. Tomorrow, I _____ (write) a letter to my uncle in Morocco.

✦ COMMUNICATIVE ACTIVITY 2

Bingo—Find Someone Who . . .

Walk around the classroom, and ask questions to find someone who is going to do each of the actions in the boxes. Write that person's name in the box. If you get a horizontal, diagonal, or vertical line of four boxes, you get a Bingo and you win.

_____ is going to cook dinner tonight.	_____ is going to do laundry tomorrow.	_____ is going to sleep in on Saturday.	_____ is going to get an A in this class.
_____ is going to go to the park this afternoon.	_____ is going to clean his or her house this weekend.	_____ is going to graduate in a year.	_____ is going to dine at a restaurant tonight.
_____ is going to buy groceries next week.	_____ is going to see a doctor soon.	_____ is going to text his or her friend later.	_____ is going to have coffee after class.
_____ is going to study on Friday night.	_____ is going to travel to another city this month.	_____ is going to eat Indian food this week.	_____ is going to have three kids in the future.

TIME MARKERS

After some specific words called **time markers**, we don't use *will* or *be going to* to express the future. Instead, we use the simple present tense to talk about the future.

Warm-up

Work in pairs. Ask your partner what he or she will do

- after he or she leaves this class.
- when he or she gets home.
- before he or she goes to sleep tonight.

Then tell the whole class about what your partner will do.

Formation

These are some examples of time markers:

when   before   after   as soon as   as long as   unless

After the time markers, use the simple present tense.

I will pay off my student loan **when I graduate**. (correct)
I will pay off my student loan **when I will graduate**. (incorrect)

After I **find** a job, I will buy a house. (correct)
After I **will find** a job, I will buy a house. (incorrect)

As soon as I **buy** a house, I will get married. (correct)
As soon as I **will buy** a house, I will get married. (incorrect)

I will travel a lot **before** I **have** kids. (correct)
I will travel a lot **before** I **will have** kids. (incorrect)

I will work **as long as** I **enjoy it**. (correct)
I will work **as long as** I will **enjoy it**. (incorrect)

I will retire **unless** I **don't have** enough money. (correct)
I will retire **unless** I **won't have** enough money. (incorrect)

EXERCISE 5

Fill in the blanks with the correct form of the verbs in parentheses.

I will tell you a secret as long as you _____ (tell, negative) anyone.

I will tell you a secret as long as you <u>don't tell</u> anyone.

1. Ryan will have driving lessons before he _____ (**take**) the driving test.

2. We _____ (**go, not**) to the park unless it stops raining.

3. I'll lend her some money as long as she _____ (**give**) it back next week.

4. They will have some coffee after they _____ (**eat**) dinner.

5. When Liam gets back home, he _____ (**call**) his friend.

6. We will email you as soon as we _____ (**arrive**).

7. After Rihna finishes her degree, she _____ (**go**) on a trip to Pakistan.

8. You won't pass this course unless you _____ (**study**) hard.

9. She _____ (**be**) happy when her friends come over tonight.

10. _____ you _____ (**help**) me when I need you?

❖ COMMUNICATIVE ACTIVITY 3

Phone Messages

🔊 Track 15

COMPREHENSION

Listen to the audio. Answer the questions.

Phone message 1

1. Why is Pablo calling Ivan?

   _____

2. When will Pablo call Ivan back?

   _____

Phone message 2

3. When is Mr. Adams's appointment?

   _____

4. What will Dr. Yu do when Mr. Adams comes to see her?

   _____

Phone message 3

5. Why is Kendra late for her meeting with Sonia?

   _____

6. When will Kendra leave work?

   _____

BRINGING IT ALL TOGETHER

❖ COMMUNICATIVE ACTIVITY 4

Role-Play

Work in pairs. Prepare a role-play for each situation. Then perform them in front of the class.

Situation A: You are stuck in traffic. Call your spouse to tell him or her that you will be late for dinner.

Situation B: Your friend is moving to a new house this weekend. He or she calls you to ask for help with the move. Make plans.

Situation C: You have a doctor's appointment and can't go to class tomorrow. Call your teacher and explain your situation. Ask for homework and about the possibility to meet with the teacher the following day.

 # COMMUNICATIVE ACTIVITY 5

Dictation

Work in pairs. Your teacher will give each pair some sentences that express the future. Dictate them to your partner. Your partner will write the sentences on a separate sheet of paper. When you and your partner finish, check for mistakes and correct them.

 # COMMUNICATIVE ACTIVITY 6

Agendas and Plans

Work in pairs. Look at the following agenda pages. On a separate sheet of paper, write sentences to describe what Angela, Erik, and Stephan's plans are. Use *will* and *be going to*.

1. Angela's To Do List

September 14	
10:00	go to doctor's appointment
1:00	attend English class
4:00	meet with Kate for coffee
7:00	after supper, call parents

2. Erik's To Do List

December 23	
9:00	finish packing
10:00	buy last Christmas gifts
2:00	take train to Toronto
6:00	call Pat before train arrives
9:00	go out with Pat and Moe

3. Stephan's To Do List

June 15	
8:00	have breakfast with Mary
11:00	pay bills
2:00–4:00	study for the final math exam
8:00	celebrate the end of the school year

Reading

Read the passage and answer the questions that follow.

NEW YEAR'S RESOLUTIONS

Often, New Year's Eve makes us reflect on the past year and think about the future. As a result, it might also <u>inspire</u> us to do something to change our looks, habits, or future in general. On this day or around this time, a lot of people make New Year's resolutions. Resolutions are like goals. Among some popular ones are to exercise more, to eat healthy food, to be organized, to <u>quit</u> bad habits, or in the case of many students, to do better in school.

If you ever want to make a New Year's resolution, you will see that following that resolution will be difficult. One of two things will happen. You will either <u>persist</u> and succeed, or you will not keep your resolution and fail. Here are a few tips that can help you follow through on your resolution.

First, to reach your goal, you will need to have <u>strategies</u>. It's good if you know how you are going to do the things you plan to do. You will need to write those strategies down. A written plan is going to help you focus on your goal.

Once you have a plan, you will finally take action and <u>commit</u> to what you want to achieve. There will probably be days when you feel like <u>giving up</u>. Therefore, to succeed, you will need a lot of motivation. Also, when you don't feel like continuing, it will be good if you let a few friends know about your resolution. In hard times, they will <u>support</u> you and encourage you to go on.

It will be a <u>challenge</u> for sure, but in the end you will be happy and proud of yourself.

COMPREHENSION

Answer the questions. Use complete sentences.

1. On New Year's Eve, why do people often decide to change something about themselves?

   _____

2. Find another word for *resolutions*.

   _____

3. Give some examples of New Year's resolutions.

4. What will you need to do if you want to reach your goal?

5. Why do you think a written plan will help you focus on your goal?

6. What will you need to do next after you have your plan?

7. Why is it good to let your friends know that you made a resolution?

ANALYZING THE READING PASSAGE

Read the passage again and <u>underline</u> all the uses of *will* and *be going to*.

DISCUSSION

Will you ever make a New Year's resolution? If yes, what will it be? If not, why not?

Listening

🔊 Track 16

WHAT ARE YOUR GOALS?

Listen to the audio. You will hear three people each talk about themselves and their aspirations for the future.

COMPREHENSION

Listen again, then fill in the chart below.

Questions	Person 1: Makila	Person 2: Renata	Person 3: Hans
1. What will this person do in the next year?			
2. What are this person's goals for the next five years?			
3. How will he or she achieve these goals?			
4. What does he or she say about the future?			

Writing

Write a short composition (maximum 150 words) about your future goals.

CHAPTER REVIEW

Summary

- There are two verb formations that we can use to express a future action: *will* and *be going to*.
- Use *will* for spontaneous or probable actions and for predictions.
- Use *be going to* for planned or intended future actions, as well as for predictions.
- After time markers, use the simple present tense and not *will* or *be going to*.

EXERCISE 1

Circle the letter of the correct word or phrase to complete the sentences.

1. _____ they go to the fair next week?
   a) Are
   b) Will
   c) Do

2. The tea is still hot. I _____ a few minutes.
   a) will to wait
   b) going to wait
   c) am going to wait

3. I'll give you a call _____ I get back from work.
   a) until
   b) when
   c) while

4. We don't have much money, so we probably _____ any souvenirs.
   a) won't buy
   b) buy
   c) willn't buy

5. _____ Ela and Karim going to visit us this summer?
   a) Is
   b) Will
   c) Are

EXERCISE 2

Fill in the blanks with *will* and the correct form of the verbs in parentheses.

There _____ (be) a lot of people at the festival.

There <u>will be</u> a lot of people at the festival.

1. How old _____ he _____ (**be**) next month?

2. We _____ (**have**) dinner tonight at six o'clock.

3. I _____ (**help**) you.

4. They _____ (**travel, not**) to England this summer.

EXERCISE 3

Fill in the blanks with *be going to* and the correct form of the verbs in parentheses.

I _____ (go) to a wedding this Saturday.

I <u>am going to go</u> to a wedding this Saturday.

1. They _____ (study) in our class next week.

2. The plane _____ (arrive) a little late.

3. _____ you _____ (do) homework tonight?

4. She _____ (go, not) to work tomorrow.

EXERCISE 4

Unscramble the following words and make them into sentences or questions.

be / Cassandra / here / tomorrow / will → Cassandra will be here tomorrow.

1. are / They / not / together / study / going to

   _____.

2. going to / the / eleven / Is / movie / at / start

   _____?

3. this / will / What / summer / do / you

   _____?

4. arrive / call / We / when / in Moscow / will / our parents / we

   _____.

5. winter /go / I / to / not / Calgary / next / will

   _____.

EXERCISE 5

There are six future tense errors in the following passage. Find and correct them.

Min is a very good student. He is always organized. Next Monday, he had an exam, so he are going to plan his time well. Tomorrow, for example, he wants to spend a few hours on reviewing his course notes. Then, this weekend, he will study on Saturday evening after he will come back from work. He wont go out with his friends as usual. Finally, on Sunday when he will get up, he will study all day long. He will relax only in the evening. He is going watch a movie and go to bed early.

10 Modals

OVERVIEW

- Modals are verbs that add another aspect to the action of the main verb. Some indicate tense, but that is not the main function of the modals.

- *Can* and *could* add the idea of ability to the main verb.

- *Have to* and *must* add the idea of necessity and lack of permission to the verbs.

- *Should* adds the concept of advice to the verb.

- We use *may*, *would*, *could*, and *can* with the main verbs to make polite requests and offers.

Warm-up

Work in pairs. Read the following conversation aloud. Underline the modals with a <u>single line</u> and the verbs that follow them with a <u>double line</u>.

Partner A: Would you like another piece of cake?
Partner B: I really shouldn't have another.
Partner A: You don't have to go right now, do you?
Partner B: Well, I should go soon. I have to be at work at five.
Partner A: You can stay a little longer. I can drive you to work.
Partner B: Thanks. Then I would like another piece of cake. It's delicious.

What do you think these modals add to the main verbs?

MODALS OF ABILITY

Can and *could* add the concept of ability to the main verb. *Can* shows present ability, and *could* shows past ability.

Warm-up

Work in pairs. Read the following two paragraphs. <u>Underline</u> all the verbs.

When we were younger, we did many more physical activities. I played basketball and my friend Juan did gymnastics. Now we aren't able to do those activities as well as we did back then. What did you do when you were younger that you don't do now?

When we were younger, we could do many more physical activities. I could play basketball and my friend Juan could do gymnastics. Now we can't do those activities as well as we could back then. What could you do when you were younger that you can't do now?

Read the paragraphs again. What is the difference between them? What do the modals *can* and *could* add to the second paragraph? What do you notice about the structure of the sentences with *can* and *could*?

Formation

Positive	Negative	Question	Wh- Question
Subject + Modal + Verb (+ object / complement)	Subject + Modal + Negative + Verb (+ object / complement)	Modal + Subject + Verb (+ object / complement)	Question Word + Modal + Subject + Verb (+ object / complement)
I **can** play the guitar. You **can** do it now. He **can** sing well. We **can** drive. They **can** win the race.	I **cannot** (can't) play the guitar. You **cannot** (can't) do it now. He **cannot** (can't) sing well. We **cannot** (can't) drive. They **cannot** (can't) win the race.	**Can** you play the guitar? **Can** you do it now? **Can** he sing well? **Can** we drive? **Can** they win the race?	**What** can you play? **When** can you do it? **How** can he sing? **What** can we do? **What** can they win?
I **could** play the guitar. You **could** do it then. He **could** sing well. We **could** drive. They **could** win the race.	I **could not** (couldn't) play the guitar. You **could not** (couldn't) do it then. He **could not** (couldn't) sing well. We **could not** (couldn't) drive. They **could not** (couldn't) win the race.	**Could** you play the guitar? **Could** you do it then? **Could** he sing well? **Could** we drive? **Could** they win the race?	**What** could you play? **When** could you do it? **How** could he sing? **What** could we do? **What** could they win?

Note: For a detailed explanation of how to form and use questions and negatives, refer to Chapter 11. Refer to Appendix B for more information on contractions.

- There is no need to conjugate the verbs. The form of *can* or *could* stays the same for each person.
- Note that *can* in the full form of the negative is one word—*cannot*. It's the only modal that adds *not* to create one word.

EXERCISE 1

Circle the correct modals in the parentheses to complete the sentences.

1. I really enjoy music. I (**can't** / **couldn't**) play a musical instrument, but I (**can** / **could**) sing pretty well.

2. When Frank was a young man, he (**can / could**) play hockey really well. Now that he's in his sixties, he (**can / could**) still skate, but he (**can't / couldn't**) play a full game of hockey. However, he (**can / could**) still play ball hockey with his grandchildren.

3. Samar had perfect vision until she turned 40. She (**can / could**) see things clearly near and far. Now she wears glasses, and she (**can't / couldn't**) see very much without them.

4. In the 1970s, a person (**can / could**) attend college or university for much less money than now. People also earned less money then.

5. I am not very good at cooking. How about you? (**Can/Could**) you cook well?

✵ COMMUNICATIVE ACTIVITY 1

Q&A

Work in pairs. Ask your partner about his or her present and past abilities or talents. Record the answers. Use *can* or *could*. Look at the following suggestions.

Questions	Answers
Can you play a musical instrument?	Dorota can play piano.
Could you do other activities when you were younger?	Dorota could play handball when she was younger.

MODALS OF NECESSITY AND LACK OF PERMISSION

Have to and *must* add the idea of necessity to the main verbs in positive sentences and lack of necessity or lack of permission to the main verbs in negative sentences.

Warm-up

Work in pairs. Read the conversation aloud.

Partner A: Didn't you have to go to work today?
Partner B: No, I booked it off because I must finish my sociology project by tomorrow.
Partner A: Do you have to hand it in tomorrow?
Partner B: Yes, first thing in the morning. I mustn't be late or the teacher will take off marks.

Read the conversation again, and underline the modals *have to* and *must*. What do you think they add to the meaning of the sentences? Do you notice anything unique about the structure of *have to*? Look back at the Modals of Ability section for clues.

Formation

HAVE TO

	Positive	Negative	Question	Wh- Question
	Subject + *have / has / had to* + Verb (+ object / complement)	Subject + Auxiliary + Negative + *have to* + Verb (+ object / complement)	Auxiliary + Subject + *have to* + Verb (+ object / complement)	Question Word + Auxiliary + Subject + *have to* + Verb (+ object / complement)
Present	I **have to** study tonight. You **have to** go there. He **has to** practise speaking. We **have to** work hard. They **have to** win.	I **do not** (don't) **have to** study tonight. You **do not** (don't) **have to** go there. He **does not** (doesn't) **have to** practise speaking. We **do not** (don't) **have to** work hard. They **do not** (don't) **have to** win.	**Do** you **have to** study tonight? **Do** you **have to** go there? **Does** he **have to** practise speaking? **Do** we **have to** work hard? **Do** they **have to** win?	**When** do you have to study? **Where** do you have to go? **What** does he have to practise? **How** do we have to work? **What** do they have to do?
Past	You **had to** go home.	You **did not** (didn't) **have to** go home.	**Did** you **have to** go home?	**Where** did you have to go?

- Adding the word *to* to the verb *have* changes it into a modal of necessity. *Have to* is not a true modal and therefore must follow the structure rules for the verb *have*. There are two forms in the simple present tense: *has* and *have*. You must use *do, does,* and *did* to make negative sentences and questions. It is the only modal that has two forms.
- The modal *have to* can express both present and past necessity.

MUST

Positive	Negative	Question	Wh- Question
Subject + Modal + Verb (+ object / complement)	Subject + Modal + Negative + Verb (+ object / complement)	Modal + Subject + Verb (+ object / complement)	Question Word + Modal + Subject + Verb (+ object / complement)
I **must** drive slowly. You **must** do it at home. He **must** sing. They **must** talk to the teacher.	I **must not** drive slowly. You **must not** do it at home. He **must not** sing. They **must not** talk to the teacher.	**Must** you drive slowly? **Must** you do it at home? **Must** he sing? **Must** they talk to the teacher?	**How** must you drive? **Where** must you do it? **What** must he do? **Who** must they talk to?

- The modal *must* expresses present necessity in positive sentences; *must* is a stronger, more formal way to express *have to*. *Must* expresses lack of permission in negative sentences.
- *Must* does not have a past tense form. Use *had to* for past necessity.
- The contraction for *must not* is *mustn't*.

EXERCISE 2

What ideas do *have to* and *must* add to the following sentences? Write *necessity*, *lack of necessity*, or *lack of permission* in the space provided.

She has to have surgery. <u>necessity</u>

I do not have to cook today. <u>lack of necessity</u>

Bonnie must not drive because she doesn't have a licence. <u>lack of permission</u>

1. I have to leave by 6:00. _____

2. You must not take things that don't belong to you. _____

3. I didn't have to take that course last semester. _____

4. You must arrive at the airport an hour before your flight. _____

5. He doesn't have to work tomorrow. _____

EXERCISE 3

Fill in the blanks with the correct form of *have to* or *must*.

When I lived at home, I _____ do some chores on Saturdays.

When I lived at home, I <u>had to</u> do some chores on Saturdays.

1. Sami _____ (negative) leave so early. He has the day off tomorrow.

2. _____ you _____ do as much homework when you took this course last year?

3. You _____ (negative) drink alcohol then drive. It's against the law.

4. Philippe _____ finish his assignment by Thursday.

5. We _____ (negative) go to school tomorrow. It's a holiday.

✦ COMMUNICATIVE ACTIVITY 2

To Do or Not to Do

Work in pairs. Make a list of actions that are necessary, that are not necessary, and that are prohibited. Use *have to*, *must*, *don't have to*, and *must not* in complete sentences. Compare your lists with those of other pairs. An example of each type of action follows.

Necessary: I have to do a load of laundry. I don't have any clean clothes to wear.

Not necessary: I don't have to withdraw any money. I have enough cash in my wallet.

Prohibited: You mustn't park here. It's a fire route.

MODALS OF ADVICE

Should adds the concept of giving advice to the main verb.

Warm-up

Work in pairs. Read the conversation out loud.

Partner A: Why are you limping?
Partner B: I twisted my ankle playing soccer. It's my own fault. I was wearing sandals. I shouldn't wear sandals to play a sport like soccer, I know.
Partner A: You're right. You should wear running shoes or soccer shoes to play soccer. I think you should go to the doctor's office or the emergency room. It looks like you should get an X-ray.

Underline *should* and *shouldn't*. What idea do you think *should* and *shouldn't* add to these sentences?

Formation

Positive	Negative	Question	Wh- Question
Subject + Modal + Verb (+ object / complement)	Subject + Modal + Negative + Verb (+ object / complement)	Modal + Subject + Verb (+ object / complement)	Question Word + Modal + Subject + Verb (+ object / complement)
I **should** leave by 10:00.	I **should not** (shouldn't) leave by 10:00.	**Should** you leave by 10:00?	**When** should you leave?
You **should** do it.	You **should not** (shouldn't) do it.	**Should** you do it?	**Who** should do it?
He **should** lose weight.	He **should not** (shouldn't) lose weight.	**Should** he lose weight?	**Why** should he lose weight?
We **should** study.	We **should not** (shouldn't) study.	**Should** we study?	**What** should we do?
They **should** go to the party.	They **should not** (shouldn't) go to the party.	**Should** they go to the party?	**Where** should they go?

There is only one form of *should*; it stays the same for each person.

EXERCISE 4

Unscramble the following words and make them into sentences or questions.

our friends / visit / on the weekend / should / we

We should visit our friends on the weekend.

1. if / should / doctor / are / to / You / go / you / the / sick

   _____.

2. on / we / to / Saturday / Should / the / go / party

   _____?

3. stop / doctor / I / smoking / My / said / should

   _____.

4. stay / or / I / I / go / Should / should

   _____?

5. really / more / for / We / study / the / should / test

   _____.

 ## COMMUNICATIVE ACTIVITY 3

Dear Know-it-all

Many newspapers have advice columns. Work in small groups. First, work by yourself to write a short letter to the Dear Know-it-all column, asking for advice about a problem. It can be funny or serious. Exchange letters with your group members. Write a response to the letter, giving your advice about how to solve the problem. Use *should*.

Dear Know-it-all,

My friend thinks it's okay to talk on his phone at the movies. He doesn't seem to understand when people around him get angry. How should I explain it to him?

Help.

MODALS FOR POLITE REQUESTS, PERMISSION, OFFERS, AND DESIRE

Warm-up

Work in pairs. Read the conversation on the next page out loud.

Partner A: May I help you?

Partner B: Yes. I'm looking for a pair of winter boots, size 8.

Partner A: We have a good selection over here, and these ones are on sale this week.

Partner B: Could I try on this pair?

Partner A: Certainly.

Partner B: They're perfect. I'll take them. Can I pay by debit?

Partner A: Sure. Would you like your receipt in the bag?

Partner B: Yes. Thanks.

Underline the modals.

Formation

These modals indicate different levels of formality, especially in polite requests.

may	most polite or formal
would	↑
could	↑
can	most informal

There is only one form for each of *may*, *would*, *could*, and *can*. These modals stay the same for each person. However, they are mainly used with *I*, *we*, and *you* for polite requests and permission.

Modal	Polite Requests	Permission
may	May I leave?	Yes, you may leave.
	May I help you?	Yes, you may help me.
would	Would you tell me more about your vacation?	
	Would you pass the salt please?	
could	Could you help me?	
	Could you tell me the time?	
can	Can I use that?	Yes, you can use that.
	Can I have another piece?	Yes, you can have another piece.
	Offers	**Desire**
would like	Would you like another cup of coffee?	Yes, I would like another cup of coffee.
	Would you like to go to the movies?	Yes, I would like to go to the movies.

- Never use *may you* in a question.
- Polite requests are in question form.
- You can express permission in a question or a statement form.
- *Would* used alone expresses polite requests.
- *Would* used with *like* (*like to* with a verb) expresses offers or desire.

EXERCISE 5

Circle the correct modals in the parentheses to complete the sentences.

1. Good afternoon. (**May / Would**) I help you?

2. (**Could / May / Would**) you like to make an appointment to see the doctor?

3. (**Could / May**) you close the window?

4. I (**could / may / would**) like to buy a ticket to Toronto.

5. (**May / Would**) we leave early? We have an appointment.

EXERCISE 6

Change each of the following impolite statements or questions into a polite request, an expression of polite desire, or an offer. There is often more than one way to express it.

Do you want some help? → **May I help you?** or **Would you like some help?**

1. Give me the salt.

   _____

2. Do you want some juice?

   _____

3. Give me your notebook.

   _____

4. I want to use your washroom.

   _____

5. What do you want?

   _____

COMMUNICATIVE ACTIVITY 4

Role-Play

Work in pairs. Prepare role-plays for the following situations. Use the polite request formations. Take turns asking and answering the questions. Then perform them in front of the class.

- Ask your partner to give you directions to the library.
- Ask your partner to help you with your homework assignment.
- Ask your partner if he or she needs help with the homework.
- Ask your partner to join you for lunch.
- Ask your partner to help you do something outside of the classroom.
- Ask your partner if he or she would help organize a party for the class.

BRINGING IT ALL TOGETHER

 COMMUNICATIVE ACTIVITY 5

Scrambled Parts

Work in teams. Your teacher will give each team five sets of cards. Each set has all the parts of a sentence on separate cards. Put the parts of each sentence together in the correct order. The team that finishes first wins.

 COMMUNICATIVE ACTIVITY 6

Role-Play

Work in pairs. Prepare role-plays for the following situations. Then perform them in front of the class.

Situation A
Partner A: You are a doctor. Your patient has diabetes. You give him or her some advice about diet and exercise and ask him to make an appointment with the dietitian.
Partner B: You are a patient. Your doctor just told you that you have diabetes. You love fast food and sweet desserts, and you don't get much exercise.

Situation B
Partner A: You took a trip to Europe (or somewhere else) last summer. Your friend (Partner B) is going there this summer. Give him or her some advice about where to go, where to stay while there, and so on.
Partner B: You're planning a trip to Europe (or somewhere else) this summer. Your friend (Partner A) went there last summer. Ask him or her for some information.

Reading

Read the passage and answer the questions that follow.

WORKING AND STUDYING

Studying at college or university in Canada can be <u>expensive</u>. Most students look for full-time jobs during the summer months and use their <u>savings</u> to pay some of the cost of continuing their education. However, more and more students feel they have to work at part-time jobs during the school year so that they can support themselves while they are studying. Four <u>decades</u> ago, only one in four post-secondary students worked part-time from September to May. Now, more than 50 percent of full-time students work part-time during the school year.

According to Statistics Canada, Canadian students work an average of 16 hours a week and earn around $6,000 during the academic year. Also, 96 percent of those students work in the <u>service industry</u>. Their jobs include work in restaurants, retail stores, and grocery stores. Because students have to match their school and work schedules, these are the kinds of jobs that can <u>accommodate</u> them. Students usually work evenings and weekends. The fact that individuals don't have to have a lot of experience to get some of these jobs is another reason for the large number of students working in the service sector.

Although many of the part-time jobs that students have seem to be <u>unrelated</u> to their studies, there are some <u>benefits</u>. Students can earn some money while they are studying. They can also <u>gain</u> some valuable experience and skills that will possibly help them start the careers they want when they graduate.

Adapted from these sources: Sam Audrey, "Students Working More, Studying Less?"; Katherine Marshall, "Employment Patterns of Postsecondary Students"; Sylvie Ouellette, "Study: How Students Fund Their Postsecondary Education."

COMPREHENSION

Answer the questions. Use complete sentences.

1. What do most students use to pay for some of their education?

   _____

2. Do many students think they need to work part-time during the school year? Why?

   _____

3. How many students worked part-time during the school year 40 years ago?

_____

4. What kinds of part-time jobs do the majority of students have?

_____

5. Give two reasons why so many students work in the service industry.

_____

6. What are two benefits of having a part-time job while you are studying?

_____

ANALYZING THE READING PASSAGE

Read the passage again, and <u>underline</u> the modals.

DISCUSSION

Do you think students should work part-time while they are studying full-time? Explain your answer.

Listening

◀)) Track 17

INTERVIEW WITH A COLLEGE COUNSELLOR

Listen to the audio. Then match the questions and answers below.

COMPREHENSION

Match each numbered question with the correct lettered answer.

1. Who is David Williams?   a) money

2. What do students have to balance?   b) school results and health

3. What do students worry about?   c) organize their time

4. What can being too stressed affect?   d) to relax

5. What is the first thing a student should look for? e) studying and working

6. What does a regular work schedule help students to do? f) a college counsellor

7. How should students treat their studies?   g) other ways to pay for school

8. What should students make time for?   h) like a job

Writing

Write a short composition (maximum 150 words) about your opinion on full-time students working at part-time jobs. Use the modals studied in this chapter.

CHAPTER REVIEW

Summary

- Modals are verbs that add another aspect to the action of the main verb.
- *Can* adds the idea of present ability and *could* adds the idea of past ability to the verb.
- *Have to* and *must* add the idea of necessity and lack of permission to the verbs. *Have to* is the only modal that has more than one form—*has to* or *have to*.
- *Should* adds the concept of advice to the main verb.
- *May*, *would*, *could*, and *can,* used with the main verb, express polite requests and offers. They are mainly in a question form. You can use *may* for permission in both statement and question forms.
- *Would like* expresses desire.

EXERCISE 1

Rewrite the following passage. Use *should* to replace the words **in bold**. Add *you* when necessary.

Before you change a light fixture, you **need to** shut off the power supply. **It's a good idea to** check that you have all of the necessary tools ready. First, you **need to** disconnect the old fixture. **It's really important to** keep all of the wires from touching each other. **The** next **step is to** connect the wires of the new fixture to the correct wires. **It's important to** make sure the connections are tight. Then you **need to** attach the fixture to the ceiling or wall. Finally, you need to turn on the power supply and try out the new light.

_____

_____

_____

_____

EXERCISE 2

Which concepts do the modals add to the following sentences? Write *ability*, *advice*, *polite request*, *offer*, *desire*, *necessity*, *lack of necessity*, or *lack of permission* in the space provided.

Would you like to come for a visit? _____offer_____

1. We have to do our homework. _____

2. May I help you look for something? _____

3. You should come to the picnic. We'll have fun. _____

4. You mustn't eat in the computer lab. _____

5. Jorge would like to learn to play the guitar. _____

6. I don't have to do it, but I want to. _____

7. He couldn't fix his car by himself. _____

8. You should ask someone to help you. _____

9. Could you tell me how to do it? _____

10. Your friend can speak Spanish very well. _____

EXERCISE 3

Rewrite the following sentences. Use modals to replace the words **in bold**.

It's necessary for you to pay your bills on time.

You must pay your bills on time. or **You have to** pay your bills on time.

1. **It would be a good idea for us to** study together.

    _____

2. Xavier **has the ability to** play the trumpet quite well.

    _____

3. **Do you want** some pizza?

    _____

4. **It's against the law for you to** drive a car without a licence.

    _____

5. **It's not necessary for Guillermo to** work tomorrow.

    _____

EXERCISE 4

There are five modal errors in the following paragraph. Find and correct them.

When you are applying for a job, you should to do some research about the company and the kinds of positions that are available. You has to revise your resumé and cover letter to reflect the needs of the position you would like to get. In addition, your resumé and cover letter must'nt have any errors. If you get an interview, you must also prepare for that. You should practise answering the kinds of questions the employer will ask. You don't have memorize your answers, but you should feel comfortable with them. You should always to dress appropriately and be confident.

EXERCISE 5

Fill in the blanks to correctly complete the sentences. Use the modals from the list. Use each modal only once.

can	can't	should	shouldn't	has to	didn't have to	would

A: Hey, Charles! _____ you like to go to the concert tonight?

B: Sure, but what about Amanda?

A: She _____ make it. She caught the flu and _____ stay in bed.

B: That's too bad. _____ you stay home with her?

A: I offered, but she said I _____ stay.

B: How much was the ticket?

A: I'm not sure. Amanda gave them to me for my birthday.

B: Okay, then I _____ go to the bank, so I _____ buy the drinks at the concert.

11 Questions, Negatives, and Short Answers

OVERVIEW

To communicate with others, you need to be able to ask and answer questions of all types: positive and negative, spoken and written.

- This chapter reviews question and negative formation and introduces short answers for all the verb tenses and modals learned in this level.

- In yes / no and wh- question formation, the auxiliary verb, the modal, or *be* comes before the subject. If the main verb in the statement form is only one word, you need to use an auxiliary verb, except for the main verb *be*.

- In negative sentence formation, *not* goes after the auxiliary verb, the modal, or *be*. If the main verb in the positive sentence is only one word, you need to use an auxiliary verb. The main verb *be* is the exception; never use the auxiliary *do* with *be*.

- In short answers, use the first word of the verb in the question—the auxiliary, the modal, or *be*—to create the short answer: *Yes* + subject + auxiliary / modal / *be* or *No* + subject + auxiliary / modal / *be* + *not*.

Warm-up

Work in pairs. Read the following conversation aloud.

Partner A: Hi. How was your trip to Mexico?
Partner B: It was great.
Partner A: When did you get back?
Partner B: We didn't get back until late last night. Our flight was delayed for 18 hours.
Partner A: Was it delayed because of the storms?
Partner B: Yes, it was. But Mexico was fantastic!
Partner A: Do you have time to get a coffee and to tell me about it?
Partner B: I don't right now. I have to get to class. Don't you have a class now too?
Partner A: Oh, yes, I do. Would you like to get together later?
Partner B: Yes, I would. Where do you want to meet?
Partner A: At the coffee shop near your place.
Partner B: Great idea! I'll see you there around five.

Write the questions and sentences from the conversation under the correct headings. Note: Do not include these in the chart: "Hi," "At the coffee shop near your place," and "Great idea!".

Yes / No Questions	Wh- Questions	Positive Sentences	Negative Sentences	Short Answers

Do you recognize any patterns? What do you notice about the short answers?

QUESTIONS WITH SIMPLE TENSES

Warm-up

Work in pairs. Read this set of questions:

Did Oleg call you last night?

Was he at work at the time?

Does he want to buy your TV?

Is it still for sale?

Will he call you tomorrow?

<u>Underline</u> the first word of the verb and the main verb in each question. What pattern do you notice?

Formation

QUESTIONS IN THE SIMPLE PRESENT AND SIMPLE PAST—ALL VERBS EXCEPT *BE*

Review the formation chart for simple present in Chapter 3 and the chart for simple past in Chapter 5.

Positive	Question	Wh- Question
Subject + Verb (+ object / complement)	Auxiliary + Subject + Verb (+ object / complement)	Question Word + Auxiliary + Subject + Verb (+ object / complement)
Simple Present		
I **like** music.	**Do** you **like** music?	**What** do you like?
You **want** to study.	**Do** you **want** to study?	**What** do you want to do?
Guy **enjoys** reading to relax.	**Does** Guy **enjoy** reading to relax?	**Why** does Guy enjoy reading?
It **has** two bedrooms.	**Does** it **have** two bedrooms?	**How many** bedrooms does it have?
We **do** the dishes together.	**Do** you **do** the dishes together?	**How** do you do the dishes?
They **work** in the evening.	**Do** they **work** in the evening?	**When** do they work?
Simple Past		
You **stayed** until 3:00.	**Did** you **stay** until 3:00?	**How long** did you stay?
He **ate** at 7:00.	**Did** he **eat** at 7:00?	**When** did he eat?
We **went** to the movies.	**Did** you **go** to the movies?	**Who** went to the movies?
They **did** their homework.	**Did** they **do** their homework?	**What** did they do?

- There are two forms of the verb *do* in the simple present: *do* and *does*. *Does* is only for the third-person singular—*he*, *she*, or *it*.
- *Did* is the only form of the verb *do* for all persons in the simple past.
- In questions, use the auxiliary *do* or *does* in the present and *did* in the past and the base form of the main verb.
- The *-s* for the third-person singular is only on the auxiliary, not on the main verb. There is no *-ed* on the main verb.

QUESTIONS IN THE SIMPLE PRESENT AND SIMPLE PAST—*BE*

In yes / no question formation, *be* comes before the subject.

Positive	Question	Wh- Question
Subject + Verb + Complement	Verb + Subject + Complement	Question Word + Verb + Subject (+ complement)
Simple Present		
I **am** sad.	**Are** you sad?	**Why** are you sad?
You **are** 20.	**Are** you 20?	**How old** are you?
It **is** very cold.	**Is** it very cold?	**How** is it?
Simple Past		
I **was** sick yesterday.	**Were** you sick yesterday?	**When** were you sick?
You **were** at home.	**Were** you at home?	**Where** were you?
He **was** here.	**Was** he here?	**Where** was he?

- *Be* has three forms in the simple present (*am*, *is*, and *are*).
- *Be* has two forms in the simple past (*was* and *were*).
- *Be* always changes its position with the subject to form questions. Never use the auxiliary *do* or *did* with the verb *be*.

QUESTIONS WITH PROGRESSIVE TENSES

QUESTIONS IN THE PRESENT PROGRESSIVE AND PAST PROGRESSIVE

Review the formation chart for the present progressive in Chapter 4 and the chart for the past progressive in Chapter 6.

Formation

Positive	Question	Wh- Question
Subject + *be* + Verb *-ing* (+ object / complement)	*be* + Subject + Verb *-ing* (+ object / complement)	Question Word + *be* + Subject + Verb *-ing* (+ object / complement)
Present Progressive		
I **am reading** a book.	**Are** you **reading** a book?	**What** are you reading?
It **is wagging** its tail.	**Is** it **wagging** its tail?	**What** is it doing?
We **are going** to work.	**Are** you **going** to work?	**Where** are you going?
Past Progressive		
I **was dancing**.	**Were** you **dancing**?	**What** were you doing?
She **was talking** to her friends.	**Was** she **talking** to her friends?	**Who** was she talking to?
They **were doing** their homework.	**Were** they **doing** their homework?	**What** were they doing?

- We form the progressive tenses with the verb *be*, so they have to follow the rules for *be*.
- *Be* always changes its position with the subject to form questions. Never use the auxiliary *do* with the verb *be*.

COMMUNICATIVE ACTIVITY 1

What Do You See?

Work in pairs. Look at the picture here. First, write five yes / no questions about what **is happening** in the picture. Use the present progressive. Second, pretend the actions in the picture happened two weeks ago. Write five yes / no questions about what **was happening**. Use the past progressive. Try to use different actions. Compare your questions with another pair's questions.

QUESTIONS WITH FUTURE TENSES

In yes / no question formation, the auxiliary verb, or *be*, comes before the subject.

They are going to leave at 9:00.

Are they going to leave at 9:00?

Review the formation charts for *will* and *be going to* in Chapter 9, pages 148 and 152–153.

Formation

Positive	Question	Wh- Question
Subject + Auxiliary + Verb (+ object / complement)	Auxiliary + Subject + Verb (+ object / complement)	Question Word + Auxiliary + Subject + Verb (+ object / complement)
Questions Using *Will*		
You **will** need some money.	**Will** you need some money?	**What** will you need?
He **will** stay.	**Will** he stay?	**What** will he do?
They **will** be tired.	**Will** they be tired?	**Why** will they be tired?
Questions Using *Be Going To*		
I **am going to** go.	**Are** you **going to** go?	**What** are you going to do?
It **is going to** be okay.	**Is** it **going to** be okay?	**How** is it going to be?
We **are going to** meet them there at Tim Hortons.	**Are** we **going to** meet them there?	**Where** are we going to meet them?

- Questions with *will:* There are two words in the verb (*will* + verb base form), so to form questions, the auxiliary *will* changes its position with the subject.
- Questions with *be going to*: To form questions, *be* always changes its position with the subject.
- Never use the auxiliary *do* with *will* or *be*.

COMMUNICATIVE ACTIVITY 2

Fortune Teller

A fortune teller is someone who claims to be able to tell what's going to happen in another person's future.

Work in pairs. Take turns playing the role of a fortune teller. Ask the fortune teller questions about your future. The fortune teller must answer, telling you about your future. Use the future tense with *will* and *be going to*. Then switch roles. Have fun!

QUESTIONS USING MODALS

Review the formation charts for modals in Chapter 10, on pages 165, 167, 169, and 171.

Formation

Positive	Question	Wh- Question
Subject + Modal + Verb (+ object / complement)	Modal + Subject + Verb (+ object / complement)	Question Word + Modal + Subject + Verb (+ object / complement)
I **can** swim.	**Can** you swim?	**What** can you do?
You **could** run faster 10 years ago.	**Could** you run faster 10 years ago?	**How** could you run 10 years ago?
He **should** try to relax.	**Should** he try to relax?	**What** should he try to do?
She **may** leave at 10:00.	**May** she leave at 10:00?	**When** may she leave?
It **would** be nice to join them.	**Would** it be nice to join them?	**What** would it be nice to do?
We **would** like to help.	**Would** you like to help?	**What** would you like to do?
They **must** go to the store.	**Must** they go to the store?	**Where** must they go?
You **have to** make dinner.	**Do** you **have to** make dinner?	**What** do you have to make?
He **has to** fix the car.	**Does** he **have to** fix the car?	**Who** has to fix the car?
We **had to** pay the bill.	**Did** we **have to** pay the bill?	**What** did we have to pay?

- All the modals except *have to* have only one form for all persons.
- Because there are two words in the verb structure (modal + verb base form), the modal changes its position with the subject to form questions.
- Never use the auxiliary *do* with modal verbs except with the modal *have to*.
- *Have to* must follow the structure rules for the verb *have*. There are two forms in the present tense: *has* and *have*.
- You must use *do*, *does*, and *did* to make questions with *have to* in the simple present and the simple past.

EXERCISE 1

Change each of the following sentences into a yes / no question.

We **took** the bus to Toronto. → **Did** you **take** the bus to Toronto?

He **can speak** English well. → **Can** he **speak** English well?

1. Marianna was baking a cake for the party.

   _____?

2. They went to the market first thing in the morning.

   _____?

3. We have to study for our test tonight.

   _____?

4. Pietra is going to meet us at the movie theatre.

   _____?

5. I should tell him about the advertisement I saw in the paper.

   _____?

6. Those students are in my biology class.

   _____?

7. His friend can play the trombone really well.

   _____?

8. She drives to school every day.

   _____?

9. We will catch the train at 8:00.

   _____?

10. Mr. Dubec taught English in Japan.

_____ ?

WH- QUESTIONS

In wh- questions, the question word asks about a specific part of the sentence. The question formation is verb (auxiliary or modal or *be*) + subject + verb, except when the question word replaces the subject.

Warm-up

Work in pairs. Read the following questions and answers.

Where is the book?   The book is on the table.
What is on the table?   The book is on the table.
When will Jan arrive home?   Jan will arrive home at 7:00.
Who will arrive home at 7:00?   Jan will arrive home at 7:00.
How many books do you have?   I have three books.

Circle the words in the answers that the question words ask for. Read the questions again. Underline the main verbs and any auxiliary verbs in the questions. What pattern do you notice in the order of the subjects and verbs? What is different about the fourth question?

Formation

Question words ask about a specific piece of information in a sentence.

Question Word	Use to Ask About	Example Sentences	
		Positive Sentence	**Wh- Question**
what	animals, things, or actions	Ian bought **a puppy**. I have **a new car**. Mariko **is studying**.	What did Ian buy? What do you have? What is Mariko doing?
who	people	He should see **a doctor**.	Who should he see?
when	time	The train leaves **at 6:00**.	When does the train leave?
where	place	We have to go **to class**.	Where do we have to go?

Continued

Question Word	Use to Ask About	Example Sentences	
		Positive Sentence	Wh- Question
why	reason	She went home **to study**. Carlos is going to stay home **because he is sick**.	Why did she go home? Why is Carlos going to stay home?
how	manner, state (health)	It was **cold** last night.	How was it last night?
how many	quantity with countable nouns	There were **four** books.	How many books were there?
how much	quantity with non-countable nouns	You have **enough** money.	How much money do you have?
how far	distance	We are **10 kilometres** from home.	How far are we from home?
how long	duration of time	The students will have **20 minutes** to finish the test.	How long will the students have to finish the test?

QUESTIONS ABOUT THE VERB OR ACTION

What asks about actions.

Positive Sentence	Wh- Question
Mariko **is studying**.	What **is** Mariko **doing**?
Frank **works** every Saturday.	What **does** Frank **do** every Saturday?
I **visited** my grandparents during the holidays.	What **did** you **do** during the holidays?
Sheena **will graduate** in June.	What **will** Sheena **do** in June?

Use the usual question word order—verb (auxiliary or modal or *be*) + subject + verb—but replace the main verb with the verb *do*.

Do must be in the same tense as the verb it is replacing.

QUESTIONS ABOUT THE SUBJECT

Positive Sentence	Wh- Question
Raj was washing his car.	**Who** was washing his car?
Anna likes chocolate.	**Who** likes chocolate?
Lightning hit the tree.	**What** hit the tree?
The book is on the table.	**What** is on the table?

When the question words *who* or *what* ask about the subject of the sentence, the question word replaces the subject, and the rest of the sentence (the verb and object / complement) stays in the same order (question word + verb + object / complement).

QUESTIONS WITH *HOW MANY* AND *HOW MUCH*

Positive Sentence	Wh- Question
There were **four** books.	**How many books** were there?
I have **two** tests tomorrow.	**How many tests** do you have tomorrow?
You have **enough** money.	**How much money** do you have?
We do **a lot of** homework after class.	**How much homework** do you do after class?

How many and *how much* replace information about specific nouns or noun phrases in the sentence. You must place those nouns or noun phrases that relate to the missing information after the question words. For example, you have to say *"How many books were there?"* not *"How many were there books?"*

EXERCISE 2

Change each of the following sentences into a wh- question. The information you want to ask about is underlined and **in bold**.

Sofia likes **to go dancing.** → **What** does Sofia like **to do?**

My brother is playing music **at a club.** → **Where** is your brother playing music?

1. His plane arrived **at 9:30**.

    _____?

2. There are **20** students in our class.

    _____?

3. I must remember to call **Julio** this evening.

    _____?

4. Francesca has to **get up** at 6:00.

    _____?

5. The students were studying **to prepare for their exam**.

    _____?

6. **Angelo** works from 5:00 to 10:00 on Friday evenings.

   _____?

7. My parents took a trip **to Brazil** last year.

   _____?

8. I'm feeling **better** today.

   _____?

9. We have **a lot of** homework to do tonight.

   _____?

10. **Too much fast food** can be bad for your health.

   _____?

NEGATIVE SENTENCES

In negative sentence formation, *not* goes after the first word of the verb—the auxiliary, the modal, or *be*. If there is only one word of the main verb, it needs an auxiliary verb. The exception is the main verb *be*.

Warm-up

Work in pairs. Read each pair of sentences.

(a) I have to get eight hours of sleep to feel rested.

I do not have to get eight hours of sleep to feel rested.

(b) Jacques will meet us at nine.

Jacques will not meet us at nine.

(c) Ali was at home last night.

Ali was not at home last night.

Underline the verbs and (circle) the negative words. What do you notice about the sentence structure?

Formation

Review the formation charts for the simple present in Chapter 3 and the charts for the simple past on pages 77, 81, and 83 in Chapter 5.

SIMPLE PRESENT AND SIMPLE PAST—ALL VERBS EXCEPT *BE*

Positive	Negative
Subject + Verb (+ object / complement)	Subject + Auxiliary + Negative + Verb (+ object / complement)
Simple Present	
I **like** to skate.	I **do not** (don't) **like** to skate.
It **has** many good points.	It **does not** (doesn't) **have** many good points.
We **travel** together.	We **do not** (don't) **travel** together.
Simple Past	
I **watched** TV.	I **did not** (didn't) **watch** TV.
He **spoke** to his friend.	He **did not** (didn't) **speak** to his friend.

- To create a negative sentence, you must use the auxiliary verb *do* or *does* in the present and *did* in the past.
- *Not* comes after the auxiliary verb.

SIMPLE PRESENT AND SIMPLE PAST—*BE*

Positive	Negative
Subject + Verb + Complement	Subject + Verb + Negative + Complement
Simple Present	
I **am** tired.	I **am not** (I'm not) tired.
You **are** a student.	You **are not** (aren't) a student.
He **is** funny.	He **is not** (isn't) funny.
Simple Past	
I **was** at home yesterday.	I **was not** (wasn't) at home yesterday.
You **were** in Haiti.	You **were not** (weren't) in Haiti.
She **was** with her classmates.	She **was not** (wasn't) with her classmates.

Be does not need an auxiliary verb, so the negative word *not* comes after *be*.

PRESENT PROGRESSIVE AND PAST PROGRESSIVE

Review the formation chart for the present progressive on pages 58 and 59 in Chapter 4 and the chart for the past progressive on page 93 in Chapter 6.

Positive	Negative
Subject + *be* + Verb-*ing* (+ object / complement)	Subject + *be* + Negative + Verb-*ing* (+ object / complement)
Present Progressive	
He **is playing** the guitar.	He **is not** (isn't) **playing** the guitar.
We **are working** in the garden.	We **are not** (aren't) **working** in the garden.
Past Progressive	
I **was listening** to music.	I **was not** (wasn't) **listening** to music.
They **were waiting** for their friends.	They **were not** (weren't) **waiting** for their friends.

- We use the verb *be* to form the progressive tenses, so we have to follow the rules for *be*.
- Place *not* after *be* to form negatives. Never use the auxiliary *do* with the verb *be*.

FUTURE WITH *WILL* AND *BE GOING TO*

Review the formation charts for the simple future and *be* + *going to* on pages 149 and 152–153 in Chapter 9.

Positive	Negative
will	
Subject + Auxiliary + Verb (+ object / complement)	Subject + Auxiliary + Negative + Verb (+ object / complement)
I **will** go. Juan **will** take the dog for a walk. They **will** try to catch the next bus.	I **will not** (won't) go. Juan **will not** (won't) take the dog for a walk. They **will not** (won't) try to catch the next bus.

be going to

Subject + *be* + *Going to* + Verb (+ object / complement)	Subject + *be* + Negative + *going to* + Verb (+ object / complement)
I **am going to** do that tomorrow. She **is going to** look for it. We **are going to** celebrate tonight.	I **am not** (I'm not) **going** to do that tomorrow. She **is not** (isn't) **going to** look for it. We **are not** (aren't) **going to** celebrate tonight.

- When there are two or more verb words, *not* comes immediately after the first word of the verb (*will* or *be*) to form the negative.
- *Not* always appears immediately after *be* to form negatives.

MODALS

Review the formation charts for modals in Chapter 10.

Positive	Negative
Subject + Modal + Verb (+ object / complement)	Subject + Modal + Negative + Verb (+ object / complement)
I **can** speak Spanish.	I **cannot** (can't) speak Spanish.
They **must** leave early.	They **must not** (mustn't) leave early.

- *Not* comes immediately after the modal to form the negative.
- Remember that *can* and *not* form one word: *cannot*.

PRESENT AND PAST WITH *HAVE TO*

Positive	Negative
Subject + *have / has/ had to* + Verb (+ object / complement)	Subject + Auxiliary + Negative + *have to* + Verb (+ object / complement)
I **have to** go home.	I **do not** (don't) **have to** go home.
He **has to** ask for permission.	He **does not** (doesn't) **have to** ask for permission.
They **had to** buy food.	They **did not** (didn't) **have to** buy food.

- *Have to* must follow the structure rules for the verb *have*. Use *do*, *does*, and *did* to make negative sentences.
- Never use the auxiliary *do* with the other modal verbs.

EXERCISE 3

Change the following positive sentences into the negative.

Eli can play basketball very well. → Eli cannot (can't) play basketball very well.

1. The children were playing in the park.

   _____

2. She should exercise more.

   _____

3. We drove to Montreal on Friday.

   _____

4. Eric is always late for class.

   _____

5. Some of the employees will organize the company party.

   _____

6. I had to do a lot of cleaning on the weekend.

   _____

7. Those students eat lunch in the cafeteria.

   _____

8. The dog broke the flower vase.

   _____

9. Yan is going to take a trip to Spain next year.

   _____

10. He wants to be a doctor.

    _____

Change and Exchange

Work in pairs. Your teacher will dictate six positive sentences. Each of you will write them on a separate sheet of paper. Compare your sentences with your partner's. Correct any errors. Next, rewrite the positive sentences as negative sentences. Compare and revise the negative sentences. Raise your hand as soon as you finish. The first pair to finish with the correct sentences wins.

SHORT ANSWERS

To create a short answer to a yes / no question, use only the first word of the verb— the auxiliary, the modal, or *be*: *Yes* + subject + auxiliary / modal / *be* or *No* + subject + auxiliary / modal / *be* + *not*.

Warm-up

Work in pairs. Read the dialogue aloud.

Partner A: Did you go to Tran's party on Saturday?
Partner B: No, I didn't. I had to work. Were there a lot of our friends at the party?
Partner A: Yes, there were. It was a lot of fun.
Partner B: It's Fidel's birthday next week. Is he going to have a party?
Partner A: Yes, he is. Are you going to be able to come to that one?
Partner B: Yes, I am. I'm going to ask my boss for the day off.
Partner A: Does he usually let you have time off?
Partner B: Yes, he does. Well, sometimes he doesn't.
Partner A: Well, I hope he does this time.

Read the dialogue again. <u>Underline</u> all the verbs. What do you notice about the verbs used in the short answers?

Formation

Question	Short Answer	
Do you like to watch sports?	Yes, I **do**.	No, I **don't**.
Does he work on Saturdays?	Yes, he **does**.	No, he **doesn't**.
Did they arrive in time?	Yes, they **did**.	No, they **didn't**.
Are you cold?	Yes, I **am**.	No, I'm **not**.

Continued

Question	Short Answer	
Am I late?	Yes, you **are**.	No, you **aren't**.
Is she from Singapore?	Yes, she **is**.	No, she **isn't**.
Were you at the concert?	Yes, I **was**.	No, I **wasn't**.
Was the boy riding his bike?	Yes, he **was**.	No, he **wasn't**.
Is it going to rain tomorrow?	Yes, it **is**.	No, it **isn't**.
Will the train leave on time?	Yes, it **will**.	No, it **won't**.
Can she speak Russian?	Yes, she **can**.	No, she **can't**.
Would you like some tea?	Yes, I **would**.	No, I **wouldn't**.
Does he have to work tonight?	Yes, he **does**.	No, he **doesn't**.

- The first word—the auxiliary, the modal, or *be*—in the yes / no question is the only part of the verb that appears in the short answer.
- The only form that changes is the verb *be* when the question is about *you* or *I*.
- Remember that *am* and *not* cannot form a contraction. I am not. → I'm not.

EXERCISE 4

Answer the following questions using short answers in the positive and the negative.

Did you go to visit your family last weekend? → Yes, I **did**.   No, I **didn't**.

Is Amalia cooking dinner? → Yes, she **is**.   No, she **isn't**.

1. Could your uncle play soccer when he was young?

   Yes, _____   No, _____

2. Do you have any brothers or sisters?

   Yes, _____   No, _____

3. Were you sleeping when I called?

   Yes, _____   No, _____

4. Do we have to write a composition today?

   Yes, _____   No, _____

5. Will the students study in the library tomorrow?

   Yes, _____   No, _____

6. Should we buy the tickets today?

   Yes, _____   No, _____

7. Are you from El Salvador?

   Yes, _____   No, _____

8. Did Tran and his sister move into their new apartment on Saturday?

   Yes, _____   No, _____

9. Are the friends going to take a trip during the vacation?

   Yes, _____   No, _____

10. Did you eat the last piece of cake?

   Yes, _____   No, _____

BRINGING IT ALL TOGETHER

COMMUNICATIVE ACTIVITY 4

Scrambled Parts

Work in teams. Your teacher will give each team five sets of cards. Each set has all the parts of a negative sentence or a question on separate cards. Put the parts of each sentence or question together in the correct order. The team that finishes first wins.

Reading

Read the passage and answer the questions that follow.

BUYER BEWARE

Whether you are buying new or used products online or a used car, you should do your homework. "Buyer <u>beware</u>" is an expression that means that you should be <u>cautious</u> when making that purchase. If the price of something seems too good to be true, it is very possible that it is just that—too good to be true.

If you like to shop online, be careful. Read all the details very carefully. There may be <u>hidden</u> charges for shipping, <u>warranty</u> services, or airport surcharges on travel packages. Compare the product with other online or real or in-store products. Also, check the security of the site if you are paying online. You don't want to put your credit card <u>at risk</u>.

If you are buying a used car, you need to do your research. Make sure you get a copy of the vehicle history. That document tells you how many owners there were and, most importantly, if the vehicle was involved in any accidents. Always get a mechanic you <u>trust</u> to check out the vehicle before you hand over any money. If the advertisement says "as is," that usually means there are things that need to be fixed and the owner doesn't want to fix them. It makes you think that the car is not <u>worth</u> fixing. Make sure you know the real cost of buying a vehicle before you buy it.

Buying online or in person can be <u>tricky</u>. Do your homework, ask lots of questions, consult some experts, and buyer beware.

COMPREHENSION

Read the passage again. Write five questions (yes / no or wh- questions) about the reading passage. Exchange your questions with another student, and answer each other's questions.

1. _____?

2. _____?

3. _____?

4. _____?

5. _____?

DISCUSSION

Do you buy products online, from newspaper ads, or from online used article sites? Do you like the convenience of buying things that way? Are you careful? Do you have any advice for others?

Listening

🔊 Track 18

APARTMENT FOR RENT

Listen to the audio. The caller is inquiring about an apartment for rent.

COMPREHENSION

Answer the following questions.

1. Which apartment is the caller asking about? _____

2. Where is the bus stop? _____

3. How much is the rent? _____

4. What is included in the rent? _____

5. What must the renter pay on top of the rent? _____

6. What floor is the apartment on? _____

7. Where is the laundry room? _____

8. How much is the security deposit? _____

9. What is the caller's phone number? _____

10. When will the caller go to see the apartment? _____

Writing

Choose a famous person, living or dead. Write a brief description of that person. Write five questions you would like to ask that individual, if you could, and explain why you would like to ask those questions. The composition should be approximately 150 words.

CHAPTER REVIEW

Summary

- In yes / no and wh- question formation, the first word of the verb—the auxiliary, the modal, or *be*—comes before the subject: auxiliary / modal / *be* + subject + verb.
- If the main verb in the statement form is only one word, you must use an auxiliary verb. The main verb *be* is the exception.
- *Be* always changes its position with the subject to change statements into questions. Never use the auxiliary *do* with the verb *be*.
- Wh- question words ask about a specific piece of information in a sentence. The question formation—auxiliary / modal / *be* + subject + verb—remains the same as in yes / no questions, except when the question word replaces the subject.
- In negative sentence formation, if the main verb is only one word, it needs an auxiliary. The exception is the main verb *be*. *Not* goes after the first word of the verb: auxiliary / modal / *be* + *not* + subject + verb.
- The first word—the auxiliary, the modal, or *be*—in a yes / no question is the only part of the verb that appears in a short answer.

EXERCISE 1

Change each of the following sentences into a yes / no question.

John should go to the doctor. → Should John go to the doctor?

1. The referee skated onto the ice. _____?

2. We were playing cards when he called. _____?

3. Sam has to work on Saturday. _____?

4. The flight is going to be late. _____?

5. I would like another cup of coffee. _____?

EXERCISE 2

Change each the following statements into a wh- question. The information you want to ask about is underlined and **in bold**.

They have **enough** time to get there. → **How much time** do they have to get there?

1. Mohammed **plays the piano** really well.

_____?

2. **Francine** is the new office manager. _____?

3. There are **six** apartments in the building.

_____?

4. I left school early **because I wasn't feeling well**.

_____?

5. He put the food **in the refrigerator**. _____?

EXERCISE 3

Answer the following questions. Use short answers.

Can you play the guitar?

Yes, I can. or No, I can't.

1. Do you have a favourite restaurant?   Yes, _____

2. Should we tell Marco about the problem?   No, _____

3. Are you going to the film festival next week? Yes, _____

4. Did you see what they were doing?   No, _____

5. Are the students studying for the test?   Yes, _____

Sentence Structure

OVERVIEW

In this chapter, you will learn more about sentence structure in English, about sentence types, and finally about some common sentence problems.

Warm-up

Work in pairs. Look at the jigsaw pieces below. Determine into what sequence you have to put them to create this picture.

What did you have to do to find the right sequence?

When making a puzzle, what usually happens if you put the puzzle pieces in the wrong way?

SENTENCE STRUCTURE

In English, every sentence has to have specific parts that are linked together so that the sentence can be complete, make sense, and, therefore, be grammatically correct. Those specific parts are the "parts of speech" you learned about in Chapter 1. It is also important that the parts are in the proper order.

Warm-up

Read the following sentences. Check if the words are in the correct order. If not, try to correct them.

1. Debora and Dawn are friends good.

2. They go to school together.

3. Like they their teacher.

Formation

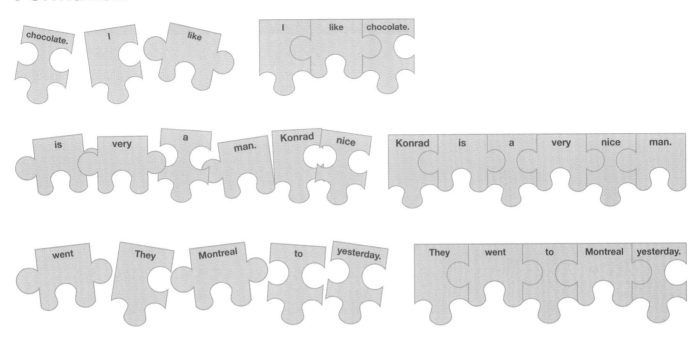

EXERCISE 1

Unscramble the following words and make them into sentences.

car / is / new / This / a   →   This is a new car.

1. beautiful / Life / is _____

2. them / visit / tomorrow / will / We

   _____

3. must / They / for / study / exam / their

   _____

4. brother / bought / last / My / a / year / house

   _____

5. needs / bread / Melissa / to / some / buy

   _____

COMMUNICATIVE ACTIVITY 1

Game—Write a Sentence!

Work in two teams. Your teacher will write several words on the board. The teams will take turns making complete sentences with the words on the board. If a team can't give a correct response in 30 seconds, the other team gets a chance to make a sentence and score a point. After several turns, the team with the highest score wins.

SENTENCE TYPES

You will learn about two sentence types here: simple and compound. Using a variety of sentence types will help make your writing more interesting.

Warm-up

Read the following two passages.

Passage 1

I am a simple person. I like simple living. Last year, my family and I decided to move to the countryside. Now, I have a healthier lifestyle. I also have more time for my family. I really enjoy living away from the city. Sometimes it is difficult. In the future, we will buy a dairy farm. Our other option is to buy land to grow crops. I encourage everyone to try to live his or her life simply. You can do it by moving to the countryside. You can also do it by living simply in the city.

Passage 2

I am a simple person. I like simple living, so last year my family and I decided to move to the countryside. Now, I have a healthier lifestyle, and I also have more time for my family. I really enjoy living away from the city, but sometimes it is difficult. In the future, we will buy a dairy farm or a piece of land to grow crops. I encourage everyone to try to live his or her life simply. You can do it by moving to the countryside, or you can also do it by living simply in the city.

Both passages contain the same information. Which passage sounds better? Why do you think so?

Formation

A **simple sentence** has the most basic sentence structure. It contains a single independent statement called a clause. A clause has a subject and a verb, and sometimes includes an object / complement.

She reads. (independent clause)
subject verb

She reads many books per month. (independent clause)
subject verb   object / complement

A **compound sentence** contains two independent statements or clauses. These clauses are joined by a coordinating conjunction. Some of the coordinating conjunctions are *and, but, so,* and *or*. When making a compound sentence, use a comma before the coordinating conjunction.

Use *and* to join clauses that have similar ideas:

My husband doesn't play hockey. (independent clause)

My daughter doesn't play hockey. (independent clause)

My husband doesn't play hockey, and my daughter doesn't play hockey. (compound sentence)

Use *but* to link clauses that express opposite ideas:

I don't like horror movies. (independent clause)

I like comedies. (independent clause)

I don't like horror movies, but I like comedies. (compound sentence)

Use *so* to show a consequence:

Aaron was sick last week. (independent clause)

He didn't come to class. (independent clause)

Aaron was sick last week, so he didn't come to class. (compound sentence)

Use *or* to indicate options:

We can go to the movies. (independent clause)

We can rent a movie. (independent clause)

We can go to the movies, or we can rent a movie. (compound sentence)

EXERCISE 2

Identify the following sentences as simple or compound.

Monique has to appraise the house. <u>simple</u>

Monique has to appraise the house and list it on the market. <u>compound</u>

1. Brittney called Shawn, but he wasn't home. _____

2. I can play the piano, and I can play the violin. _____

3. The bank opens at nine o'clock. _____

4. They don't have enough money, so they can't go to Mexico this summer. _____

5. Jakub is smart and handsome. _____

EXERCISE 3

Fill in the blanks with the correct coordinating conjunction: *and, but, so,* or *or*.

Our neighbours are farmers, _____ they have to wake up early every morning.

Our neighbours are farmers, <u>so</u> they have to wake up early every morning.

1. Grace likes to draw, _____ her sister likes to draw too.

2. It was a rainy day yesterday, _____ I stayed home.

3. They went to the party, _____ they didn't like it.

4. My friend needs a new car. He will get a part-time job, _____ he will borrow some money from his parents.

5. The students studied hard for the test, _____ they all passed it.

❖❖ COMMUNICATIVE ACTIVITY 2

What Type of Sentence Is It?

Work in pairs. In the following paragraph, underline all the simple sentences with a <u>single line</u> and all the compound sentences with a <u>double line</u>. (Circle) all the conjunctions.

Some people actually like having complex lives and constant drama in their lives. It's their personality, so they wouldn't enjoy simple living. Instead, they prefer to be on the go or to meet with people, and they often like to work a lot too. The ongoing business keeps them motivated and happy. It might be hard to believe, but such people can still find time to stop and rest in their busy lives.

SENTENCE PROBLEMS

Sentences that are incomplete or joined in the wrong way are incorrect and, therefore, ungrammatical. They make reading confusing. To write well, you need to know what sentence problems look like and how to correct them. The two main types are fragments and run-on sentences.

Warm-up

Your teacher will write several sentences on paper strips and cut them into individual words. You will receive one word. Find the classmates whose words can combine with yours to create a complete sentence. Write your sentence on the board.

Formation

Fragments are incomplete sentences. They are missing an important part, or they just finish without a complete idea.

I like. (fragment)	I like English. (sentence)
She driving. (fragment)	She is driving. (sentence)
Because he is tired. (fragment)	He stayed home because he is tired. (sentence)

To avoid a fragment, test the sentence by asking these questions:

- Does it include a verb?
- Does it have a subject?
- Does the sentence express a complete idea?

Run-on sentences are composed of two sentences that use the wrong punctuation mark or are not joined with a conjunction.

We like our teacher, she is very sympathetic. (run-on sentence)

We like our teacher. She is very sympathetic. or We like our teacher; she is very sympathetic. (correct sentences)

He missed the bus, he still got to class on time. (run-on sentence)

He missed the bus, **but** he still got to class on time. (correct sentence)

To fix run-on sentences, do any of the following:

- Place a period (.) between the two complete sentences.
- Place a semicolon (;) between the two complete sentences.
- Place a comma (,) and a conjunction between the two complete sentences.

EXERCISE 4

Read the following sentences. Next to each sentence, write C if the sentence is correct. If the sentence is incorrect, identify whether it is a fragment (F) or a run-on sentence (RO), and then correct it.

Adam has. (F) → Correction: Adam has a great sense of humour.

1. I can't help you I am busy. _____

2. She would like to travel around the world. _____

3. My professor nice. _____

4. Talk to me after class. _____

5. They will check the answers, then they will correct their mistakes. _____

6. If you want to succeed. _____

7. We took a lot of photos during our trip to Netherlands. _____

8. It belongs to her, it's not yours. _____

9. He likes Japanese cars. For example, Toyotas. _____

10. Nadia doesn't have to work tonight, so she'll go out with her friends. _____

✠ COMMUNICATIVE ACTIVITY 3

Newspaper Headlines

Newspaper headlines are often written as fragments and not complete sentences. Work in pairs. Read the following newspaper headlines, and try to guess what the complete sentence might be.

- The gold medal for Canada in women's 100 metres
- The neighbourhood restored
- Brave teenager
- All because of his talent
- Waiting for help

BRINGING IT ALL TOGETHER

✠ COMMUNICATIVE ACTIVITY 4

Game—Join the Sentences

Work in teams of two. The teacher will give you and your partner paper strips with different sentences. You will have five minutes to combine your sentences with your partner's sentences using the correct conjunctions. Write the sentences in the space provided. The team with the highest number of correctly combined sentences wins.

_____

_____

_____

_____

✠ COMMUNICATIVE ACTIVITY 5

Role-Play

Work in pairs. Prepare a role-play for the following situations. Then perform them in front of the class.

Situation A: Your best friend has a problem. He or she wants to visit a cousin in another province but doesn't have a car. Offer him or her different options. Use conjunctions to link your sentences.

Situation B: Your co-worker asks you for help. There are things that you can help him or her with. However, you also believe that there are things that are his or her responsibility and not yours. State your opinion. Use simple and compound sentences.

COMMUNICATIVE ACTIVITY 6

Mini Oral Presentation

Work in pairs. Make four sentences that describe your and your partner's abilities. For each sentence, use a different conjunction. Then, you and your partner will present the sentences to the rest of the class.

COMMUNICATIVE ACTIVITY 7

Quotations

Work in pairs. Read the following quotations. Identify whether each quotation is written using a simple sentence (S) or a compound sentence (C). Circle the correct letter. Then discuss the quotations.

Sometimes good things fall apart, so better things can fall together.   S C
— Marilyn Monroe

Ships in harbour are safe, but that's not what ships are built for.   S C
— John Shedd

The grand essentials of happiness are: something to do, something to love, and something to hope for.   S C
— Allan K. Chalmers

Happiness is not the absence of problems; it's the ability to deal with them.   S C
— Steve Maraboli

Life can only be understood backwards, but it has to be lived forwards.   S C
— Stuart Connelly

Ability can take you to the top, but it takes character to keep you there.   S C
— Zig Ziglar

Life's a marathon, not a sprint.   S C
— Phillip C. McGraw

Each moment spent on this bright blue planet is precious, so use it carefully.   S C
— Santosh Kalwar

We need no language to laugh.   S C
— Janaki Sooriyarachchi

Reading

Read the passage on the next page and answer the questions that follow.

JIGSAW PUZZLES

A jigsaw puzzle is a puzzle, and as with every puzzle, you need a solution to it. The solution or end result of a jigsaw puzzle is to make a complete picture by <u>reassembling</u> its many small pieces. Often, these puzzle pieces are of different shapes, but each piece usually has a part of a picture on it. That makes it easier to determine what pieces go together. When all the pieces are in their correct spots, a jigsaw puzzle is complete and <u>reveals</u> the entire picture.

The origins of jigsaw puzzles go back to around 1760. People created these puzzles by painting a picture on a flat piece of wood, and then cutting that picture into small pieces with a special wood cutting tool called a jigsaw. These days, jigsaw puzzles are made <u>primarily</u> on cardboard. That way, they are easier and cheaper to produce.

Jigsaw puzzles typically come in many sizes, <u>ranging</u> from 100 to 1,000 pieces. Children's puzzles are usually smaller. There are also family puzzles, three-dimensional jigsaw puzzles, and even computer versions of jigsaw puzzles. You can find all <u>sorts</u> of images on jigsaw puzzles. The most typical ones are nature scenes, animals, and buildings. However, you can even turn your photos into puzzles. Some people, after completing a puzzle, glue it to another <u>surface</u> and hang it on the wall to serve as a decoration.

Doing puzzles is a great pastime activity and educational tool not only for kids but for adults too. You can use them to help your child to develop spatial skills. You can also introduce puzzles at community centres, work <u>retreats</u>, family reunions, or parties as a way to make a group of people work as a team. Doing puzzles can even help people relieve stress, learn how to concentrate, and keep their brain active.

Next time you are looking for an activity to do by yourself or as a group, try out a jigsaw puzzle. It's lots of fun!

COMPREHENSION

Answer the questions below. Write complete sentences.

1. What happens when you put all the jigsaw puzzle pieces together?

   _____

2. At first, what material did people use to make jigsaw puzzles?

   _____

3. What tool did people use to cut a picture into small pieces?

   _____

4. What do we make jigsaw puzzles from today? Why is this material used?

_____

5. What images do we usually find on jigsaw puzzles?

_____

6. How big can jigsaw puzzles be?

_____

7. According to the text, what are some benefits of doing jigsaw puzzles?

_____

DISCUSSION

- Do you remember doing puzzles when you were young? Do you do puzzles these days?
- The text gives you some benefits of doing jigsaw puzzles. Do you think there could be some disadvantages of doing puzzles too? Give examples.

Listening

🔊 Track 19

THE ART OF BROKEN VASES

Listen to the audio.

COMPREHENSION

Answer the following questions.

1. Why was Melodie absent from school yesterday?

_____

2. What happened as she was carrying the box?

_____

3. What was inside the box? Why was it precious to her?

_____

4. What was the subject of the lesson in the last art class?

_____

5. What was Liam's solution to Melodie's problem?

_____

Writing

Write a short composition (maximum 150 words) describing one of the following:

- a location that is special to you
- your favourite pet
- your best friend
- your car or the car of your dream

In your description, use different types of sentences: simple and compound. Make sure to use conjunctions too. Proofread your text for fragments or run-on sentences, and then correct them.

CHAPTER REVIEW

Summary

- The proper sentence structure makes your writing complete, grammatically correct, and therefore easy for the reader to follow.
- If you want your writing to be more effective, use both simple and compound sentences.
- A simple sentence contains one clause with a subject, a verb, and sometimes an object or a complement.
- A compound sentence contains two clauses that we join together with a conjunction.
- The four main conjunctions are *and*, *but*, *or*, and *so*.
- To avoid sentence fragments or run-on sentences, check that your sentences are complete and either connected well by the correct conjunction or separated by the correct punctuation mark.

EXERCISE 1

Match the numbered first part of each sentence in Column A with the lettered second part of the sentence in Column B.

Column A	Column B
1. Howard likes to dance,	a) but she wasn't there.
2. The movie was	b) we have lots of homework to do.
3. My roommate forgot his key,	c) and Libby likes to dance too.
4. Clara and Felix	d) his dog.
5. I called my friend,	e) were very tasty.
6. You can give it to me,	f) will move to Vancouver next year.
7. We need to leave now;	g) but I was home.
8. He takes good care of	h) is looking for a job.
9. The cookies	i) or you can leave it with her.
10. Jinny	j) really good.

EXERCISE 2

The following paragraph uses simple sentences. In the space provided, rewrite the text. Use compound sentences whenever possible. Don't forget the correct conjunctions and punctuation marks.

We link individual words to make a sentence. Similarly, we connect two or more links to make a chain. Chain was invented in 225 BCE. People used it to draw a water bucket from a well. Back then, they made chain with metal rings. These days, we also use other materials to make chains. Presently, we use the concept of a chain for many articles. We use it in tools, such as chainsaws. We also use it in bicycles. We even use it in jewellery, such as necklaces and bracelets.

_____

_____

_____

_____

_____

_____

_____

EXERCISE 3

There are five errors with sentence structure in the following passage. They are <u>underlined</u> for you. Correct them.

Some <u>people think technology</u> can simplify your life. <u>and</u> others think it can make life even more complex. Many of us use technology on an everyday <u>basis but</u> this might not mean it's always good for us. For example, we might benefit greatly when it comes to cars, cellphones, and <u>computers, they</u> save us a great amount of time, <u>or</u> at the same time, they can sometimes be "stealing" our precious time. Some of us also have to admit that we are addicted to technology, and we can't live without it. <u>It a</u> controversial topic.

EXERCISE 4

Circle the letter of the correct word or phrase to complete the sentences.

1. Eddie got an A on the test, _____ he was very happy.
   a) and
   b) but
   c) so

2. Nicole grows her own vegetables, _____ she eats them every day.
   a) and
   b) but
   c) or

3. She is always in a hurry, _____ she loves it.
   a) and
   b) but
   c) so

4. I like to sit in front of a fireplace and to look at the flames.
   This is an example of a _____.
   a) simple sentence
   b) compound sentence

5. Because it's relaxing.
   This is an example of a _____.
   a) fragment
   b) run-on sentence

Part 3 Review

Self-Study

OVERVIEW

The self-assessments in this unit give you a chance to review and reinforce the grammar points from Part 3 (Chapters 9–12).

Check your knowledge and if you find areas that need more attention, go back to the appropriate chapter and review the material.

EXERCISE 1

Unscramble the following words and make them into sentences or questions.

this / am / I / work / going to / summer → I am going to work this summer.

1. must / early / I / tomorrow / get up

   _____.

2. after / going to / you / What / do / dinner/ are

   _____?

3. have / Identical / do / twins / identical / not / fingerprints

   _____.

4. a / Can / change / tire/ you

   _____?

5. poisonous / Avocados / to /are / birds

   _____.

6. , but / The / was / she / difficult / it / test / passed

   _____.

7. sunny / It / be / this / will / weekend

   _____.

8. taking / Were / the / notes / students

   _____?

9. our / learn / We / from / should / mistakes

   _____.

10. you / Why / have / now / to / do / leave

   _____?

EXERCISE 2

Change each of the following positive sentences into the negative.

Martin Cooper was the first person to make a cellphone call on April 3, 1973.

Martin Cooper was not the first person to make a cellphone call on April 3, 1973.

1. You should have an annual medical checkup.

   _____

2. A blue whale's heart is the size of a Volkswagen Beetle.

_____

3. During your lifetime, you'll eat about 27,000 kilograms of food.

_____

4. Ancient Egyptians slept on pillows made of stone.

_____

5. Forensic scientists can determine a person's sex, age, and race by examining a single strand of hair.

_____

EXERCISE 3

Change each of the following sentences into a yes / no question. Then give a short answer to each question in the positive and in the negative.

People are about one centimetre taller in the morning than in the evening.

Are people about one centimetre taller in the morning than in the evening?

Yes, they are.   No, they aren't.

1. We have to protect our environment.

_____?

Yes, _____.   No, _____.

2. Space tourism will be common in the near future.

_____?

Yes, _____.   No, _____.

3. Timothy was working when it happened.

_____?

Yes, _____.   No, _____.

4. You can make change for a dollar in 293 ways.

_____?

Yes, _____.   No, _____.

5. Women's hearts beat faster than men's.

_____?

Yes, _____.   No, _____.

EXERCISE 4

Change each of the following statements into a Wh- question. The information you want to ask about is <u>underlined</u> and **in bold**.

Ontario contains over **250 thousand** lakes. → How many lakes does Ontario contain?

1. People **in parts of Western China** put salt in their tea instead of sugar.

   _____?

2. Persia changed its name to Iran **in 1935.**

   _____?

3. **Linen** is actually stronger when wet.

   _____?

4. You have to be **16 years old** to get a driver's licence in Canada.

   _____?

5. In the future, we will communicate **by reading each other's minds.**

   _____?

EXERCISE 5

Correct the errors in the following sentences. The errors are <u>underlined</u>.

1. I did not <u>came</u> to Canada in 1991.

2. To be a successful student, you <u>might</u> study hard.

3. It's very windy<u>,</u> the storm is coming.

4. <u>Is</u> Grace and Hannah going to the summer camp next year?

5. How often does she <u>talks</u> with her mom?

6. I <u>should</u> like some tea, please.

7. The soup was too spicy, <u>and</u> I did not eat it.

8. Monarch butterflies <u>can to</u> travel up to 8,000 kilometres per year.

9. <u>Have</u> strawberries more vitamin C than oranges?

10. I <u>wont</u> be here tomorrow.

EXERCISE 6

Fill in the blanks with the correct form of the words in parentheses. Use different verb tenses, modals, and short answers.

Ten years ago, while I ₁ _____ (do) my master's degree, I ₂ _____ (learn) a lot about myself. In particular, I remember one class on Adult Learning. One day, our professor ₃ _____ (say), "In this class, you ₄ _____ (have, negative) a final exam. Instead, you ₅ _____ (write) an essay: an autobiography. To write it, you ₆ _____ (modal, advice) reflect on your life and your learning style. You ₇ _____ (modal, possibility) also use various textbooks and other scholars' theories. Your essay ₈ _____ (modal, lack of permission) be longer than 30 pages. You ₉ _____ (modal, obligation) submit it by the end of the month. ₁₀ _____ you _____ (have) any questions?"

Some of the students asked, "₁₁ _____ (modal, permission) we keep it afterward?"

He answered, "Yes, you ₁₂ _____ (modal, permission)."

It ₁₃ _____ (be, negative) an easy project, but I really ₁₄ _____ (enjoy) it. These days, I ₁₅ _____ (read) my autobiography at least once a year. It's so good that I often ₁₆ _____ (ask) myself, "₁₇ _____ I really _____ (write) it?" I proudly reply, "Yes, I ₁₈ _____ (do)."

In the future, I ₁₉ _____ (give) it to my daughter so that she ₂₀ _____ (modal, possibility) read it and learn more about her mother. I think everyone ₂₁ _____ (modal, advice) write his or her autobiography once in their lifetime. It ₂₂ _____ (be) a great tool to realize who you really ₂₃ _____ (be) in the past, who you ₂₄ _____ (be) now, and who you ₂₅ _____ (modal, possibility) become in the future.

EXERCISE 7

Find and (circle) all the words in the word search below. Copy the remaining letters from the word search into the spaces below it to find what the message says.

puzzle	conjunctions	yearbook
mosaics	intelligence	agenda
sentences	resolution	comma
question	goal	request
negative	technology	advice
modal	simple	must
adjective	complex	can
adverb	plan	and
combine	prediction	but
or	so	

```
P  C  C  O  T  C  N  C  O  M  M  A  G  R  A  T
L  U  A  L  E  R  O  M  O  S  A  I  C  S  A  T
A  P  Y  N  C  I  E  M  O  I  A  G  E  N  D  A
N  U  E  P  H  N  O  S  B  D  N  S  Y  O  C  N
U  Z  A  R  N  T  A  F  O  I  A  I  N  I  O  D
S  Z  R  E  O  E  D  H  S  L  N  L  E  D  M  N
L  L  B  D  L  L  J  R  E  Q  U  E  S  T  P  E
A  E  O  I  O  L  E  E  N  U  S  T  V  E  L  G
D  L  O  C  G  I  C  O  T  E  A  I  I  N  E  A
V  E  K  T  Y  G  T  A  E  S  D  R  M  O  X  T
I  S  G  I  E  E  I  Y  N  T  V  O  U  P  N  I
C  O  O  O  R  N  V  E  C  I  E  A  D  B  L  V
E  Y  A  N  F  C  E  O  E  O  R  R  T  U  H  E
E  N  L  E  X  E  T  L  S  N  B  E  V  T  E  L
C  O  N  J  U  N  C  T  I  O  N  S  M  U  S  T
```

Message

— — — — — — — — — — — — — — — — —!

— — —   — — — — — — — — —   — — — — —   — — —!

— — —   — — —   — — — — —   — — —   — — —

— — — —   — — — — —?

APPENDIX A: COMMON IRREGULAR VERBS

Base Form	Simple Past	Base Form	Simple Past	Base Form	Simple Past
arise	arose	go	went	shoot	shot
be	was, were	grind	ground	show	showed
beat	beat	grow	grew	shrink	shrank
become	became	hang	hung	shut	shut
begin	began	have	had	sing	sang
bend	bent	hear	heard	sink	sank
bet	bet	hide	hid	sit	sat
bind	bound	hit	hit	sleep	slept
bite	bit	hold	held	slide	slid
bleed	bled	hurt	hurt	speak	spoke
blow	blew	keep	kept	speed	sped
break	broke	kneel	knelt	spend	spent
bring	brought	know	knew	spin	spun
build	built	lay	laid	split	split
burst	burst	lead	led	spread	spread
buy	bought	leave	left	spring	sprang
catch	caught	lend	lent	stand	stood
choose	chose	let	let	steal	stole
come	came	lie	lay	stick	stuck
cost	cost	lose	lost	sting	stung
cut	cut	make	made	stink	stank
deal	dealt	mean	meant	strike	struck
dig	dug	meet	met	swear	swore
do	did	mistake	mistook	sweep	swept
draw	drew	pay	paid	swim	swam
drink	drank	put	put	swing	swung
drive	drove	prove	proved	take	took
eat	ate	quit	quit	teach	taught
fall	fell	read	read	tear	tore
feed	fed	ride	rode	tell	told
feel	felt	ring	rang	think	thought
fight	fought	rise	rose	throw	threw
find	found	run	ran	understand	understood
fly	flew	say	said	upset	upset
forbid	forbade	see	saw	wake	woke
forget	forgot	sell	sold	wear	wore
forgive	forgave	send	sent	win	won
freeze	froze	set	set	wind	wound
get	got	shake	shook	withdraw	withdrew
give	gave	shine	shone	write	wrote

APPENDIX B: CONTRACTIONS

Simple Present   We often join the verb *be* or the auxiliary verb with *not* to form contractions or shorter forms. We join the two words together and use an apostrophe (') to replace the letter *o*.

Be + *not*	Auxiliary + *not*
is not → isn't	does not → doesn't
are not → aren't	do not → don't

He is not at home right now. →
He isn't at home right now.

We do not take the bus to school. →
We don't take the bus to school.

Note: *I am not* is the exception. We make a contraction only with the pronoun *I* because a contraction with *not* is too difficult to pronounce.

I am not. → I'm not.

Simple Present—*Be*   We often join subject pronouns with a present tense form of the verb *be* to make contractions or shorter forms. The apostrophe (') replaces the missing letter.

Positive	Negative
he is → he's	he is not → he's not
she is → she's	she is not → she's not
it is → it's	it is not → it's not
we are → we're	we are not → we're not
you are → you're	you are not → you're not
they are → they're	they are not → they're not

I am not hungry. → I'm not hungry.

It is not cold today. → It's not cold today.

They are not very old. → They're not very old.

Present Progressive   Because we use the present tense of *be* to form the present progressive, we follow the same rules for forming contractions as we do for the simple present of *be*.

Be + *not* + verb *-ing*
is not going → isn't going
are not starting → aren't starting

It is not raining. → It isn't raining. or It's not raining.

We are not studying. → We aren't studying. or We're not studying.

Simple Past   We contract the verb and *not*.

Be + not	Auxiliary + not
was not → wasn't	did not → didn't
were not → weren't	

It was not late. → It wasn't late.

You were not alone. → You weren't alone.

Note: There is no contraction possible with the subject pronoun and the verb *be* in the simple past.

Past Progressive   Because we use the past tense of *be* to form the past progressive, there is **no** contraction possible with the subject pronoun and the verb *be* in the past progressive.

Be + not + verb -ing
was not watching → wasn't watching
were not doing → weren't doing

I was not dreaming. → I wasn't dreaming.

They were not driving. → They weren't driving.

Simple Future with *Will*   *Will* can form a contraction with *not*. *Will* can also form a contraction with the subject pronouns.

Will + not	Subject pronoun + will
will not → won't	I will go → I'll go

I will not go. → I won't go.

She will leave at 9:00. → She'll leave at 9:00.

She will not leave at 9:00. → She won't leave at 9:00.

Simple Future with *Be Going To*   Because we use the present tense of *be* to form the future with *be + going to*, we follow the same rules for forming contractions as we do for forming the simple present of *be*.

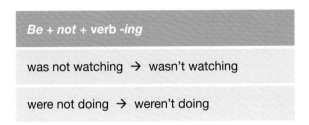

Subject pronoun + be + going to		
Be + not + going to	Positive	Negative
is not going to → isn't going to	he is going to → he's going to	he is not going to → he's not going to
are not going to → aren't going to	they are going to → they're going to	they are not going to → they're not going to

Note: *I am not* is the exception. We make a contraction only with the pronoun *I* because a contraction with *not* is too difficult to pronounce.

I am not going to study. → I'm not going to study.

He is going to study. → He's going to study.

He is not going to study. → He isn't going to study. or He's not going to study.

Modals

- We can form contractions with these modals and *not:*

Modal + *not*			
can	cannot swim → can't swim	should	should not leave → shouldn't leave
could	could not swim → couldn't swim	would	would not like → wouldn't like
must	must not go → mustn't go		

- *May not* is the exception. We cannot make a contraction with *may* and *not* because the contraction is too difficult to pronounce.

  You may use this computer. → You may not use this computer.

- We must use the auxiliary *do* with the modal *have to* in a negative sentence in the present or past, in order to make a contraction with *not* and the auxiliary.

do + negative + *have to*	
does not have to → doesn't have to	She does not have to work today. → She doesn't have to work today.
do not have to → don't have to	We do not have to write the test. → We don't have to write the test.
did not have to → didn't have to	They did not have to do that. → They didn't have to do that.

- *Would* can form a contraction with the subject pronouns but usually only in positive statements.

Subject pronoun + *would*	
he would like → he'd like	I would like to go to the concert. → I'd like to go to the concert.

APPENDIX C: MODALS

Modal	Meaning and Use	Example Sentences
can	present ability	Johan can speak several languages.
	polite request (most informal)	Can I help you?
	permission (most informal)	You can use this computer station.
could	past ability	As a young man, he could run long distances.
	polite request (informal)	Could you pass the salt please?
	permission (informal)	You could do that later.
has / have to	present and past necessity	I have to study tonight.
		He has to go to work.
		We had to leave early.
	present and past lack of necessity	You don't have to pay extra.
		He doesn't have to take lessons.
		They didn't have to attend the lecture.
may	request (most polite)	May I help you?
	permission	You may leave when you finish the assignment.
must	present necessity	I must leave by 9:30.
	present lack of permission	You mustn't drive the wrong way on a one-way street.
should	advice	You should think before you speak.
would	polite request (normal)	Would you collect all the books for me?
would like	offer	Would you like another cup of coffee?
would like to	desire	I would like to travel this summer.

GLOSSARY

Word or Term	Definition	Chapter	Page
accommodate	to make the way things happen match the needs of the people who are doing them	10	174
adopting	taking something as your own	8	136
aspect	a quality or characteristic of something	2	34
assembly line	a number of people working together to put something together as a whole, one piece at a time	3	52
at risk	in danger, not safe	11	198
become familiar with	to get to know or recognize an area, an activity, or a person	1	19
benefits (n.)	good results	10	174
beware	be careful; it might not be a good thing	11	197
campus	the area and buildings of an institution, educational or business	1	19
cautious	careful or aware that there might be problems	11	197
challenge (n.)	a difficulty; something requiring you to work hard to achieve	9	158
colonization	the act of having new people come to live and control a new area	8	136
commit	to decide to do something completely, until it is finished	9	158
confusing	not clear; possible to misunderstand	1	19
conquered	took control over someone by force	8	136
constantly	continuing without stopping	8	136
crowded (adj.)	not much space; a lot of people or things in the same space	5	86
crucial	really important or necessary	4	65
cruise (n.)	a short, organized trip usually on a boat	5	86
decades	groups of 10 years	10	174
determine	to decide or choose	4	66
display (v.)	to show or demonstrate	7	119
efficiently	in a way that uses time and resources in an economic, effective way	7	118
enhances	makes better; improves	4	65
entertainment	an activity produced by someone for the enjoyment of others	5	86
entire	whole, complete	3	51
errands	small tasks that you need to do outside of your home, such as shopping or going to the bank	3	51
escaped	gained freedom from a confined area or space	6	98
evolve	to change or develop over time	8	136
expand	to grow larger	8	136
expensive	costs a lot of money	10	174
expertise	high level of knowledge about a certain subject	2	35
extend	to give an opportunity or reach out to someone	3	52
fireworks	minor explosives set off to produce bright lights and sounds in the sky for the entertainment of others	5	86

Word or Term	Definition	Chapter	Page
gain (v.)	to get, achieve, or add to something	10	174
giving up	stopping doing something because it is too difficult	9	158
grand finale	the final part or end of a show that impresses the audience even more than the earlier parts	5	86
grateful	thankful; appreciative	6	99
guidelines (n.)	a list of instructions or ideas to follow	4	65
hidden	not clear or not easily seen, possibly on purpose or intentionally	11	198
hiring	the act of selecting and giving someone a job	2	34
incorporating	bringing different things together to become one	7	119
influences	the things, ideas, or people that make you decide to do certain things	8	136
inspire	to make you want to do the same thing and believe you can	9	158
instead of	the opposite of what was just mentioned; in place of; or not	3	52
interact	to communicate; have a two-way conversation	7	119
kinesthetic	referring to your body's movement and ability to move	7	119
lineups	people stand in lines to wait for their turn to get or do something	1	19
loaded	full of; containing a lot of	2	35
look forward to	to be very interested in what is going to happen in the future; to anticipate	3	52
obesity	the effect of being very overweight or weighing more than you should	4	65
paw (n.)	the foot of an animal, not a person, with toes	6	99
persist	to continue to do something until it's finished even if it is difficult	9	158
play-dates	times set aside for children to get together to play	3	51
predominantly	in the majority; mainly	7	119
primarily	most importantly or in the first position of importance	12	210
quality time	time that is valuable or good for the people who spend it together	3	52
quit	to stop doing something	9	158
ranging	a limited time or area for something to happen or be used	12	210
reassembling	putting something back together or in the order it is meant to be	12	210
register (v.)	to officially give information and agree to sign to do something	1	19
rely on	to be certain of; depend on; count on	2	35
renovate	to change something in a house or building to make it more up to date or more modern	2	34
retreat (n.)	activities away from the normal environment to work on new ideas or to get together with friends	12	210
reveals	shows something that wasn't easily seen before	12	210
roaring	the loud noise made by an animal or thing, such as a lion or a car engine	6	99
roots	beginnings of something; sources	8	136
savings	money that you set aside or do not use so that you can use it for a future purpose	10	174
sedentary	not active	4	65
self-esteem	how you feel about yourself	4	65

Word or Term	Definition	Chapter	Page
service industry	an area of business that serves the public, such as restaurants, hotels, entertainment, and so on	10	174
slave	someone who does not have freedom and who must do as his or her owner or master demands without pay	6	98
sorts (n.)	kinds or types	12	210
source (n.)	the original place where you found the information	2	35
souvenirs	objects to remind you of a place or an event	5	85
spatial	involving space and things within that space	7	118
stalls (n.)	partially enclosed or divided areas for displaying or containing objects, such as a vegetable stall (where one sells vegetables) or a horse stall (where a horse is contained within a building)	5	85
strategies	ways, ideas, or procedures you choose to help you do things	9	158
stuff	an informal word for things or objects in general	1	19
suffers	receives the bad effects of something, such as a disease	4	65
support (v.)	to help or give strength to something or someone	9	158
surface (n.)	the top area of a thing	12	210
swollen	increased in size because of an injury	6	99
thorn	a sharp part of a plant stem, such as on a rose	6	99
trend (n.)	the direction people are viewing and going along with; something such as a fashion trend or a way of thinking	2	35
tricky	difficult or challenging; not easy to do	11	198
trust (v.)	to have confidence in something or someone; to have the feeling that someone is not going to hurt you	11	198
tuition fees	the amount of money you have to pay for the courses you want to take	1	19
unrelated	there is no connection with a known thing	10	174
vendors	people who sell things	5	85
visualize	to bring an image to mind; to be able to see something in your mind	7	118
wandering	going from place to place without really knowing which way to go	6	98
warranty	a guarantee or an assurance that something will do what it's supposed to do for a certain amount of time	11	198
worth	the value of something; to be worth something means it is a good idea to do; there will be a benefit	11	198